MEHEN

MEHEN

The Oracle and the Time Movers

Athena Gaga

KU
PRESS

KINGSTON UNIVERSITY
PRESS

Edited by Holly Roberts and Jade Grocott

Design and Production team
Jade Grocott
Yulianna Permyakova
Lidia Trifonova
Holly Roberts

KINGSTON UNIVERSITY PRESS
Kingston University
Penrhyn Road
Kingston-upon-Thames
KT1 2EE

Mehen: The Oracle and the Time Movers

Hierophile: The Oracle of Dodona

I walk in a forest of shadows. My reality drifts like a breeze over morass weeds. It is a mundane world. Some lights uncover Nature's force. It is a sublime world. The dove. The swarm. The flock. The forest has the power to transform my steps; his name is Sellos.

In the night tears flow from his sky, burning stars the Pleiades. The Raven is here; the Eagle has left towards the East. Libya or Lebanon? No one knows where my sister lies. A voice inside me says she is dead. Floating dream. Floating island in my sleep. She comes close to me. I see her eyes, her face like a full moon. She is quiet like a lost child. In the waters of Styx, I give the oath. The River of Lamentation pours blustering streams into Acheron. She appears to me, illuminating letter. I read aloud. In every word the reality shifts; in every word my reality twists. She dances like a diamond body, swirling, arborising, a vine, the Vine. Drink she says, dream she says, give an answer she says.

They wait; the tree gazes at my lips. The Oracle they say. They wait. I am the Oracle of Dodona. This place is green like the fluid in the veins of my god. I spell three, four, five words. No more. Interpreting the Wind. Reading the Waters. Writing the Earth. Sometimes it is just a wave, a dance; my soul dances the prophecy. They wait. I pray. They wait in silence. The prayer is a song. I brought it from the desert like a rare bird. The song springs; his echo breaks time. The axis is vertical. An ascent. Like the birds' flight in the grey sky. It rains. Time surpasses the small valley, slips up the mountain running above the sea.

My homeland, I miss my homeland. Did I ever have one? The power of being resists non-being. Total surrender. Sacrifice. They bring the Lamb. I get the knife; the poor little soul looks at me, a tear of suffering, a tear in my hands, his blood on my clothes; the heart is beating alone. The Old Man rips off his skin. He reads the bones. The Book of the Dead lies on the bones. His flesh is words; his flesh conceives forgetfulness. It rains; the blood streams on the ground, my eyes resisting being. Ecstatic thunders break space, standing out of time like golden spheres. Tremendous mysteries. Save us all. It is Pentheus forest. There is no fate. A gigantic automaton. Pentheus, the no-Fate man. Dionysus comes to the stage. Honey springs from the ground. Do you like to see them? Do you like to see them? The Old Man hides his face, opening then his hands to Heaven, eyes closed. Pentheus thunders.

'The world can be resolved. A riddle. I am the no-Fate man. Pull off the chords, build up the space gluing the circles, take off the membranes, hold down the strings, fill up all the weak forces. My matrices are evolving in time. Move now, approach the facts.'

Do you like to see them? The Bull doubles; Dionysus gives him a thyrsus.

'Bend Felix king to my ground, evergreen, everlasting like a sorrow without name, like the wolf chasing the gazelle. Of the three natures mine is the one derived from a foreign thing. Evolving into my body. World evolving into my body.' *Pentheus replies.* 'The future value of the individual depends on the value of the neighboring cells. That alone can model reality. The configuration has not necessarily a pre-image.'

Dionysus bursts out laughing. 'Evolution becoming conscious of itself.'

He turns his head. Milk springs from the earth. I look at the Herdsman. He is blind. I hold him by the hand.

'He is the end, or maybe the perfection,' *I say.*

'He is just the activity,' *the Old Man replies.* 'Has being only through.'

'Through what?' *I ask.*

'An imposition, a converge; or, perhaps, another translation. Look,' *the Old Man says.* 'A minuscule change, the volume-constant changes like an arrow in time.'

I see him walking.

Troy: The Seed

This journey swells my feet. The heat causes a series of mutations, leaving them without shape. A transfiguration to some sort of reptile's legs. We have walked through this desert for twelve days now. I wonder why we have to walk. There are those villages, the villages that we have to protect, but the villages are empty. Just some thrown bricks. Steve says that he is tired of this project.

Steve: It is nonsense. The villages do not exist; we protect something that does not exist.

I don't speak. The swelling seems to move now to my belly. My belly is swollen. I try to hide it. I leave my shirt loose. I wear my jacket with open buttons. Life crumbles all over the place; it is a strange life, grains of dust and seeds. Sometimes they get into my nose. I try to sneeze them out. Steve sees me and waves his hand.

Steve: Don't try, Troy. They are already inside your lungs. No matter how much you sneeze you can't protect your lungs.

He wears a mask, like a tube; he breathes from the tube.

Steve: Troy, you have to make one for yourself.

There is one more guy in our company, Neil. Neil speaks very little; he moves like a serpent in the sand; from time to time he looks at the sky. He makes signals, rotating an iron rod that he carries at his waist. Sometimes he looks at Steve. He stares at him as though ready to punch him in the face. Steve laughs.

Neil: You, little rats. You, little beggars. I hate you. Both of you. Eiii, you, swollen face. *I touch my face.*

Me: I don't feel my face. I don't feel my face.

Neil comes near me and punches me, fist closed, straight on my nose.

Neil: Now you feel it, moron. Shut up, never say a word again. Next time I will break this stick on your face.

Neil walks near to a derelict little house. He pisses.

Neil: Bastards. Bastards. Two pieces of shit.

He approaches me again.

Neil: You breathe them; that's your problem. You have to use a tube or you fight them from inside. Fight. You understand? Refuse. Refuse them. Look.

He takes off his shirt; his belly is flat.

Neil: Look at you; you let them eat you slowly like bread. Stupid. So, fucking stupid. *I look at my hand terribly frightened.*

Neil: Yes, I have seen it. The pores are opening. Grain and seed. You are something like fertile ground to them. They come out of you like small shadowy ghosts.

Neil grabs tight hold of my hand, pricking a rusty needle to my skin. My palm hurts; small drops of blood appear.

Neil: That's it, that's it. You are not ground; no, I was mistaken. You are a playground. They play with your cells; drilling you, cutting you, ripping you, erasing you.

Neil laughs. Steve intervenes in the conversation. I look at him, searching into his eyes for help.

Steve: You are bleeding his hand with this needle. Leave him alone.

Neil frees my hand.

Steve: We go back to our basement, Troy. The whole project is nonsense. We go back, now.

Me: Back? Do you have a map? Do you know where is back and where is front? Do you know?

I watch Steve sitting down. A despairing movement. The knees do not hold despair. I know that. You have to sit down, the gravity effect, the earth, one with the earth; this is suffering.

Steve: I once had a map, I know I had one.

Me: We are lost. There is nothing we can do.
My voice neutral, no colour, soundless.
Steve: Move, Troy. Walk. We have to walk, Troy.
Me: I cannot, Steve. My feet are swollen. I can't move.
This time I hear my voice; it has something of a faint bell, this terrible grazing sound.
Steve: Look, I don't like you, but I like you better than Neil and I can't go on travelling all alone, thus you have to move as I do. Come on, walk. I will fix a tube for you and you will be fine.

I agree. I have a tube now. It helps. My breathing is getting better. We walk until the next empty village. We run into a small yellow house with a mattress thrown in the middle of the otherwise empty living room. I need some sleep. Steve goes out to speak to Neil, doesn't say about what. I lie like a sack of rotten food. My eyes are heavy. My body an unknown territory. I see her. She comes close to me; she isn't young or old, tall or short; I couldn't describe what she looks like, but she comes close to me. She touches my hand. Takes off my tube. Kisses my lips. My name, she says, is...

Hierophile: Medio Topo

The Old Man speaks slowly.
Herdsman: Do you see them?
Hierophile: Yes, they breathe the seed.
Herdsman: I know, my dear Oracle. Bythos is taking place.
We walk to the lake. A fine line is keeping the horizon like stem in her fingers. The bleeding aurora. The atmosphere has a faint pink colour. A daisy opens her petals. Twenty-four.
Herdsman: The redemption consists of freeing the higher from the lower.
Hierophile: Are they going to die?
Herdsman: No, no, only consumed. They are moving towards Omphalos, let them alone.
Hierophile: Troy is losing his mind.
I say, and I feel the sorrow's arrow breaking my heart.
Herdsman: The fool stays in rest, creating a reverie of pain. Have you seen your sister?
Hierophile: No, I haven't.
Herdsman: Liar. She is clothed with the Sun, with the Moon under her feet, and on her hand a garland of twelve Stars.

Hierophile: The dragon waits for the birth. Your apparition taking narration into Drusiana's fall. It is just a medio topo. You need to transmit the helpers.
I am talking fast, barely breathing, trying to keep my voice firm, but I am sure he knows that it is only an effort.
Herdsman: No, let them weep.
Hierophile: An entire age?
Herdsman: Only six emanations.
We move with a small boat. The sun keeps the same position avoiding setting the world in motion.
Hierophile: There is an alternative?
Herdsman: Either, my dear, you accept dualism, or you are unable to think.
Hierophile: That's a joke I suppose.
I speak hardly keeping my tears from flowing.
Hierophile: I am happy that we take separate lives in a while.
Herdsman: You are going to miss me.
The Old Man speaks slowly, making each word the sound of a distant wind; his voice though, has a velvety texture like a warm cloth over my shoulders.
Hierophile: I know, but one more mistake makes no difference.
I say abruptly, almost vengefully. I hold him by the hand, till the bridge. No goodbyes.

Hierophile: Sabbe, The Oracle of Siwa (Hierophile's Sister)

My sister's words are flying like fearful birds before the tempest.
Sabbe: I heard the words of Imhotep. Reshaping time through narration. Falling walls. My soul on my lips. A troubled journey circuiting the sun. Brute fear of injustice. Faces wiped out. Like being drunk from a promising land. I am parched with thirst and I perish. Is it Death's perfume? Like a clear sky, an ever-flowing spring. The cypress. The sky ship approaches. The flaming altar, the weary wheel. And my soul said, are you alive? I promise no peace in the West for all the coming days. No shores. Be still, my sister, until the day of offerings. Rise up from your tomb, the current leaps, the fish whisper. Blind ignorance in your pale dome. Still motion. A transfigured god. Watch over; the serpent precedes the mighty companion. He who devours men, sacrifices the first born, swallows the night fall. Twin are the heavens, shattered the bones, broken the forms. The storm is approaching. Look at the knives, steel and silver. You shall stand at the gates. Daughter of Earth and the starry Heaven. The messenger of storm, gone. Orion is imprisoned in the underworld. Stirred is my

heart. You have a purpose. Can you hear me? You have a purpose. Weep not. The land has perished but you are alive. Do not offer tears. The Re must restart creation. Remember whether you are sleeping or awakening. Remember the cypress.

Sabbe: Where are you from?

Hierophile: I am in pain.

Sabbe: They rob the birds, the birds of prayer.

Sabbe: Who are you?

Hierophile: I am in pain.

Sabbe: Let me offer you a land holy like my sickness. Worlds are falling on their heart. Let me give you a land as a rhythm, Heliopolis. Justice shall rise like a snake among the tombs. With my strong arm and in my many incarnations, like a guardian with a scarlet thread, I command you; breathe the flood, the Great Green Sea. The pomegranate is uprooted; the dear land of Egypt is the realm of your dreams. The harp sings. Beautiful is the day. Splendour scattering the hordes. Who dares to spell retreat? Re, Ptah or Atum; a trinity of unchanging forms. In the Temple of Truth, grieve not your heart whatever it comes, sweet may the music be, pure like a tree growing in the sunlight.

Then my sister slept but I had a purpose.

Troy: A misconception

I speak to Steve, trying to explain, trying to make him understand our situation.

Me: I have those dreams, my destiny or fate lying ahead of me. She told me that it is called Omphalos; we have to start walking faster. A living entity, a triggering agent spiralling inside our flesh. The events are inside us like a detrimental sense of deluded will. Hyper time curves into the nucleus. The world's clock synchronizes itself in full regression.

Steve: Your sickness accelerates Troy; you had to keep your tube. Now it is too late. We must find a wagon; we have to search for our basement. You run into madness my friend. It is the Desert's psychotic effect.

Me: No, we are enclosed. Confined. My entire body remembers.

Steve calls Neil. He looks at me like some strange fish in an aquarium.

Neil: He has fever. Give him some water to drink; don't bother with the tube, it is too late. His condition is meaningless. He either lies in a lapse of time or, more likely, it's the seed pairing inside him.

Steve: Neil, it can happen to anyone.

Neil: No just to him. His lack of boundaries results in absurdity.

Steve: For god's sake, he was just lacking a tube. It is an accidental confusion.

Neil: No. His past works; he suffers from the past. A fragmentation. A misconception contradicting his present identity.

Steve: It is the seed.

Neil: I know, but that's only a mere explanation.

Me: Stop it, please. I am getting tired of listening to both of you. You want me to walk. I will. The rest is my business.

Neil: I am not sure; maybe you could stay here. We will send help as soon as we get back to our camp.

Me: There is no camp. I am coming with you. We must walk faster.

Neil: Ok but if you cannot make it, then I am not going to wait for you. Expect no sympathy.

Me: I didn't ask for it.

Steve: How do you feel?

Me: The swelling has gone; it's like silence, a consensus; the noise has gone.

Steve: You are their host. Perhaps they don't want to kill you. You are vital to them. A ground of being.

Me: Oh, please Steve, don't speak like that. I think I am getting better. Wasn't anything so dangerous; only an allergic reaction to some seeds.

Steve says nothing, but it is obvious that he has his opinion. I don't care. The important thing is that I can go on.

Hierophile: The Pool

I was sixteen when I met my sister. She had curly, fair hair; she was wearing a fine dress of muslin and stunning leather sandals carved with figures. One strap was keeping her cloth on the shoulder and a silver necklace was shining on her chest; but she looked like a child dressed in a woman's clothes, although she was only a year younger. She gazed at me with admiration and said, 'I am happy that you are here.'

I thought that she was too intimate in her manners, but then her appearance, this babyish face, her eyes clear like a topaz, fearless like the sound of sistrum, those eyes said: 'I will never grow old.'

The Great Mother introduced us. Nobody was entering the temple without her approval. The Mother said that her name is Sabbe, but she would be known one day as the Oracle of Siwa; first though, she had to learn a few more things, practice her abilities and improve her skills. It was my turn to look at her with admiration; tenderly I touched her hand and I asked her to be my sister. She smiled and said, 'I am already your sister. I am the voice in your head, the dreams in your sleep.'

When the Mother left us alone, she said, 'Let's go to the river; show me the god's shores; show me the birds and the trees; show me the lions and the spears.'

We ran out; the river was taking a hidden path, coiling like a snake, creating a pool full of green bamboos and beautiful flowers. Water snakes and frogs were the only creatures swimming in the dark waters. She took off her clothes and went in. Her body was pale like a swarm of bees. Her kiss was sweet like a honey drop.

'You are beautiful,' she said and kissed my breasts. 'I think I love you.'

I was laughing, asking her how she could say such a heavy word so fast. She made a serious face.

'I am going to be the most precious oracle of all time, and you ask me if I know what I feel? I want to slap you but then I cannot because I love you.'

'Swim with me now. Kiss me,' she said. 'Kiss me more.'

It felt like being in a dune, sucking dust and sand and salty water. I opened my eyes. She was trembling in my hands. Since this day we were together. She was now wearing a pardalite like men priests do, painting my eyes heavily with kohl. She dressed me like a queen with a gorgerine and all her ornaments, earrings, wigs and an anklet she had from her home.

'One day I will be your only guide, one day, years later, you will sit down like an old scriber, recalling memories while the bells will break the circle of lands. One of us will be sacrificed. I have chosen it to be me.'

'You, stupid little demon,' I said, 'I hate the way you speak.'

She held my hand and said, 'I will not die my beloved sister. I will be forever the faint voice in your dreams, your beloved assistance in your duties.'

Troy: The Maze

We come close to a rocky place. Ground is coming out of earth like the thorns of the cactus. Steve looks unhappy.

Steve: This place is like a maze Troy. It changes all the time, but we don't move at all. I mean we walk but we don't move. Time seems to fly away but it's mostly like losing spacing and consequently seems like movement annihilation. Guess what, I am trying to make a map. I make those dots if we meet a village and those lines when we move to another. Each time we arrive in a village I leave a sign; all of them are so alike you can't tell the difference; three times we passed already from the same positions; there is no doubt about it. The ground changes from sandy to rocky and back again, but we are in the same place, the house with the mattress in the living room, near the rocks.

Me: Are you a con?

I walk into the little house then stop in terror; the mattress is there and my tube also. I look at Steve.

Me: Neil? Does he know?

Steve: No, not yet. I am not sure if I should let him know or how exactly to say it. It is like a coiling snake, but with no way to find where the tail or the head lies.

Me: Mehen, this is called Mehen. It's an ancient Egyptian game; unfortunately, we don't exactly know the rules. We have to split his body into sections, I think, and then to try to pass from one section to another. It seems like we have been trapped in the same section. Do you understand?

Steve: No, I don't. Look at these marbles Troy.

They are lying on the floor, three small spheres with a lion seal. I remember playing with them while half asleep when I had my fever crisis. Some sort of decorative figures, not too heavy but icy cold, not marble, probably bronze. Steve touches them.

Steve: They are hot.

I touch them. He is right. I throw them on the floor in front of me. My fingers burn. We stay there silent when Neil comes in.

Neil: We are in the same place, aren't we?

Steve: Yes.

With his iron rod Neil gives a strong hit on one of the spheres. It rises up as a feather on an unnoticed breeze and strikes softly on the wall. The earth moves like in an earthquake; the wall vanishes. The place is green, bamboo and blue lotus buds are dripping from the dark waters of the river. The water snake moves fast; the frog has no chance to escape. A faint voice in my head says, 'He will take the white crown, He will take the red crown. He will join the two mighty ones. The Son of Man will make his name for all eternity.' Probably it is the seed; it has affected us all; we hallucinate.

Hierophile: The Huntress of the Savage Goose

My sister left one morning following the orders of our Great Mother.

'Siwa will be your new dwell,' *our Mother said to Sabbe.* 'An extraordinary fate surrounds you. Siwa is only the first of your lands. Go my dear daughter and do as you are instructed to do. Dream as you are able to dream. Talk only if necessary. Never sacrifice your voice; beware the golden stream carries the forgery of a dubious present.'

I was alone for the first time. 'Huntress of the Savage Goose walk with me pathways hidden under the branches of the star domes. Care for me, my sister. Care for me.'

Fine words, beautiful like my sorrow, engraved by my sister's hand on the temple's walls. My fate was waiting for me in the city of Helios and her words were lost in the fragility of memory. Our Great Mother called me into her rooms. I was wearing a simple linen dress and my sister's anklet. My hair was nicely combed, long with ornaments and flowers swirling around it.

'My beauty,' *said our Mother.* 'Your time has come. The great city of Helios will bend under your lovely feet. The temple of Re, the granite pillars of the Atum will be your home. The On, the Pleroma of the Two Horizons are coming. The Bull doubles, waiting in a raining forest. Do not forget your sister; one day, years from now, she will be your only guide. Help them; their steps are moving in insanity. The Temple of Iniquity, the temple that folly is nesting, will give them to Mnevis. Save them. It is a homonym. The riddle; it is a homonym. Keep our book. It's a physical structure. An all-encompassing sphere.'

I bent on my knees and I said, 'my beloved Mother, am I going to see her again?'

'No,' *she said*. 'Never.'

Then she breathed, and she touched me with a golden thread tissue on my forehead. The sorrow disappeared. My sister was a beautiful bird flying in the blue sky. A dove. A beautiful dove. Our Mother smiled, and she turned her back; but I wished to ask something more and I touched her, forgetting the rule, forgetting that we never touch the Mother. I touched her. Her body shook like passing a vast change, her face now in front of mine, eyes sparkling like fires; the tail went around my body like a python around his prey. I was suffocating, falling in a deep sea, dying in a sweet and unforgivable embrace. Ecstasy. I have no other word to describe the pleasure that spread through my body.

'I love you,' *I whispered,* 'Mother.' *The spasm moved from my body to hers.*

'I am Lilith,' *she said without opening her mouth.* 'Know this, you are blessed to live my life.'

'My life,' *she repeated*, 'my life. You are my life.'

She moved slowly out of the main hall. A serpentine. For days I felt her morbid hug all over my body. Cold like a breeze of death, warm like an erotic flame, shivering inside my heart, recalling the sense of an immense abyss, recalling her.

The days passed fast; my only concealment for the two losses was the morass with the lotus flowers and the blue lilies. I was there day after day, swimming and dreaming. Snakes and frogs were my company. Doves were touching my hair with their feathers.

The last day, before my long trip to Heliopolis, I went to see my lonely shelter. I took off my clothes and fell into this beautiful water pool with closed eyes. The water was warm, like a tender flame, falling like a caress on my body. I felt the tortuous sense of a serpent coiling around my waist, looping slowly around my neck. I kept my eyes closed. Tight was the touch, like fingers keeping me from breathing, then a tuneful breeze of fresh air, a taste of myrrh on my lips; the underwater world opened in my eyes like a weave in a loom, a warp beam shedding, battening, coming into existence. I closed my eyes feeling like a nursing baby in her arms.

'Sais,' *she said*, 'Sais. Beloved like eternity. Six roots, one crown.'

A blue butterfly flew over my body, then closed her wings and lay on my umbilical. When I moved my hand to touch her, she flew away like a lost wish. I was there under a fig tree, naked and warm, happy and sad at the same moment. The sun was falling, the last beams wandered in the branches, pink, a faint pink with purple shadows, the strips of an unknown sky animal raising its pace for another land.

It was raining when I arrived in Heliopolis; the priests marvelled at the sign. The great priest Menath came to see me. 'Let the rain fall,' *he said.* 'Let the light be,' *he said.* 'The Owl and the Serpent. The shuttle and the needle. The great weaver mother of all. Six roots and one daughter. The goose and the blue lotus. Sweet might be your stay, my dear Hierophile, to the pillars of Bennu.'

Troy: The Snake

I speak carefully like I am afraid to awaken something unknowingly dangerous.

Me: She talks to me.

Neil: Shut up, Troy.

Steve: Let him speak.

Neil is playing with his rod, cropping the bamboos, chasing the snakes. His way of ignoring me does not disturb my need to speak.

Me: She says: 'the maze is alive, veiling itself in a continuous creation.'

Me: She says: 'the maze acquires cognitive faculties while occupying space.'

Me: She says: 'the maze has volition.'

Me: She says: 'you must find the entry key.'

Steve: I am tired, Troy. We probably hallucinate; we are infested. Fucking seed. I hope it is not a permanent effect. We will be fine in a while, a sort of psychedelic effect, like a drug. We will be fine; we must stay cool, not let ourselves loose. It will pass. Let's concentrate, discipline our thoughts. It will pass, just a drug effect, that's all.
Neil takes off his clothes.
Neil: Drug or not, since we have a private pool, I am going to enjoy these warm waters.
He is swimming happily like a child.
Steve: Why not? Hallucination or not, let's enjoy our stay in this paradise.
Me to Steve: Look, a fig tree.
Steve: Great, Troy! I love it. Snakes and figs, now it is time to see our Eve.

We are playing like children do with the waters. A snake comes close.

I say, 'Come on, little friend, lie on my arm.' *His head is near to mine. Water snakes are harmless, at least that is what I've heard, although for a moment fear passes through my blood. His eyes, like fire, drill into my mind.*

'Fool,' *he says without moving his mouth.* 'My unity is shattered, the map is splintered, future devours the past. Find the key or die with me.'

I feel an urgency to get out. 'The key,' *I say aloud.* 'Guys we must find the fucking key.' *The sun is falling, a faint pink.*
Steve: Any clue, Troy? What does the key look like?
Me: No, no idea.
Steve: Nice help she gives you.
Me: We don't hallucinate Steve. We are trapped. That's it. I feel like someone plays with us.
Neil, having cropped a lotus flower, starts to remove the petals. The rain is strong, a smell of salty water falls on my face; the seagull left an only feather near my feet.
Steve: This guy is lucky or knows something we don't.
I am filled with joy.
Me: What a beautiful place. I could stay here all my life.

Hierophile: Heliopolis

'I could stay here all my life.'

The city of Helios, the pillars of the Phoenix. I walked around free from any ties; happy to be alone when I wished, so happy to be with the priests when I felt like I wanted to speak. Menath placed no pressure on me. He decided though, that I had to attend the courses of the wise. He was instructing himself from time to time. Now

and again he disappeared for several days; then he was around for several weeks.
But nobody asked questions. He was the High Priest.

One day he lectured us, a team of eight students; on the variety of world systems.
He called them Life Models. I was the only woman. 'This course is very special,' he
said. 'It is the first phase to the road of mysteries. Geometry, mathematics, physics,
are nothing if not combined in the Krasis of Soul. The numbers are here only if
implemented by life. You are life to them. You must learn to live in harmony to be
able to attain full existence. Let's play a game. Here, I design a square with only two
possible states, black and white. Could you tell me, if we assume four orthogonally
adjacent squares plus the four remaining squares, how many possible black and
white combinations we have?'

That was a difficult problem. I drew down my squares and I started painting
them. All black, all white. One black, one white. Nonetheless, I couldn't find an end
number. I needed a day to do that, I thought, or even more. I started feeling anxious.

'Do we have a start colour or square?' *Tiras, one of my colleagues, asked and his*
voice showed considerable frustration. Good question, I said to myself.

Menath was laughing, 'If you wish so. Start with the white. I will see you in two
days.'

We decided to split the work among us. One student started from the first
square, first row and white colour. A second from the second square, white colour.
The third from the third square, white colour. The other three did the same but for
columns. That makes six. The remaining two, we took the diagonal lines. But we
messed it up so much that we had to eliminate similar patterns and finally, two days
later, we came up with the number of possible clusters.

'That's a ridiculous thing with which to pass our days,' *commented Mnemon,*
another of my colleagues. 'It's a job for prisoners' *he added.* 'Counting squares. Now
we counted them, what's the big deal? It's only a matter of labour, not of thought.'

As we spoke, I saw Menath coming. 'Mnemon is right,' *he said.* 'Because he
was counting like a kid instead of defining the relation among the squares and the
numbers. Our problem is to count not as punishment, but as a way to find the inner
relation. Let's say that now I give you a square that you can paint black, white and
red. Let me know the patterns.'

We looked at each other in despair. Mnemon raised his hand and said 'I get it. It
is one more state but the same square.'

Menath nodded, yes. Menath was a strange man in appearance but also in
his behaviour. He looked more like a eunuch than a man but at the same time he

was very mannerly in his ways, and no one ever heard anything which harmed his reputation. But still there was always gossiping around his disappearances.

Tiras said, 'he probably had some health issues from birth; he was deformed bodily, that's why he enjoys tormenting his students with terrible square counting.'

For a moment it crossed my mind that maybe he was right; it was impossible for me to count more squares without screaming. We left, all except Mnemon, who was the best of all of us; he wanted to prove it once more and find the relation. Menath said we could continue next week. Great, I thought, time to go to the sea. We went to the beach near to the temple; there were some girls playing with the sea foam.

'I haven't given my oath yet,' *Tiras started the conversation,* 'I am not sure actually, if it is worth the effort. Counting stupid squares, it may be better to be a scribe or something else.' *We laughed and Tiras, half insulted, half bored, left us and went to speak to the young priestesses. No one was flirting with me since I was already sacred and that meant curse and severe punishment. I didn't mind, because I didn't like anyone in particular. I think I was tied to my memories and all this flirting seemed too shallow and of no importance.*

'Nature wants offspring. Hierophile wants to see the mysteries,' *I said to myself. Did they have something of the loom I experienced in the underwater world? I was alone now; the rest of the students had left one by one to join the ceremony of the evening prayers. Menath came to the beach, a faint pink covering the great horizon, the disk of the sun hiding fast behind evaporated clouds.*

'If you would like to swim, you can,' *he said.* 'I will watch for intruders.'

'Thank you,' *I replied, dazed from his unexpectedly friendly manners.*

'I held myself with difficulty,' *I added.* 'I was waiting for the night to fall.'

'I know. You do that quite often,' *he said without a trace of discontentment in his voice.*

'It is not allowed?' *I asked, mostly to appear gentle than to get permission.*

'For you it is allowed,' *he smiled and continued.* 'You will rarely find a woman who knows how to swim in these places, but since we have an exception let's not be cruel. Enjoy the sea. I also love swimming. Thus, I can understand your need.'

'Would you like to join me?' *I asked, in a naive manner. I regretted my question immediately. That wasn't polite; that was a stupid invitation.*

'Not now, maybe later,' *he replied and looked straight into my eyes. I felt relief because I wasn't sure if I wanted to see the deformed, naked body of our Teacher. Freezing salty waters, it was April but in the evening the waters were still chilly. I recalled my pool and a wave of nostalgia fell like a curtain upon my eyes; a tear dropped from my eyelashes to the sea.*

'Do not cry,' *Menath said*. 'Time is here and now, it is always like that, there is no past, there is no future, only a formless change.'

The water was dark, but the light of the stars was enough to glimpse the Teacher's body. Tiras was right, but not exact. It wasn't deformed; it was holy. Like the body of the creator sculpted in the main entrance of the temple. But again, I took it as a metaphor, a ritual imprinting, not an actuality. I thought that was the image of a god that has both forms, including the two forces of life, male and female, a Disypostaton; what otherwise is called a Double Essence, not as a reality.

'You are right; I am the primordial form, or one of the forms.'

'You prefer this?' *he said softly. Now he looked like a great white cygnet. The Savage Goose. It was all over me, a breath of joy; then he came back to the Menath, half man, half woman. I touched him without fear.*

'In the Father's womb water lilies spring under a tomb.'

'That's a funny thought,' *he said. He came closer.*

'In the Mother's womb water lilies spring under a dome.' *I looked at him frightened. He was moving slowly from the lacuna to the Nile. A serpentine.*

'Mother,' *I screamed but she didn't look back. I stayed at the beach watching the stars shining, millions of bright flames, until I had fallen asleep.*

Troy: Theasis

I am tired like I am losing all my strength.
Me: I feel exhausted. Drained.
Neil to Me: Ok. Get some rest you fool. Steve and I will be better off you.
Neil to Steve: Let's go soldier, let's have a look; this place seems just fabulous.
We are in the movies. Steve, Neil and me. My name is Troy. We are watching in this new great Multispectrum-Theasis panoptic cinema an old movie, a remake, three soldiers moving in the dessert.

'I am bored,' *says Neil*. 'Boring subject; the end is so predictable. Let's change room spectrum.'

Steve and I agree. Again, a remake; the serpent in the lagoon, eating poor soldiers.

'Gosh,' *says Neil*, 'fucking kingdom of boredom.' *He switches spectrum*. 'Here we are. I love mummies and ancient temples.'

'Look,' *he says*. 'We can play the soldiers in the movie. I love this technology; it's just great. I will be the tough guy, kill a thousand mummies and steal the girl. Steve will be the sceptic, the quiet, compassionate and common-sense driven guy. You

Troy, you can be only what you are. The fool, the psychic that speaks to the ghosts. Lovely. I assign the roles. Ok?'

Before I answer he has done it. The idiot. I hate him. He is just a hen in the egg, playing the rough soldier, well protected from real dust or heat or whatever. I wake up dizzy. My dream. The truth is, we are in a movie, that's all; we are a squadron in the Multispectrum-Theasis panoptic cinema. I feel relaxed. Do I have to tell them? Or let Neil be, in his fantasy of the furious soldier? Why do I not see any actors? Probably the idiot didn't set up the program well; anyway, at least soon it will end, and we will go home. I try to remember where home lies but it seems impossible. It is the role; they make it look realistic, 'Forget all your anguish and life; get a couple of hours pure entertainment. Be someone else.'

Great. I don't mind. I can relax now.

Steve: Troy. Troy, wake up. Come here. Neil has been trapped.

Me: Trapped in his stupid mind? *I ask, and it feels good.*

Steve: Please Troy, it is not the time for jokes. Follow me.

I walk towards Steve. He looks upset. We move through the pillars of the temple to an open area, a beautiful square with four altars. Steve pushes me by the arm to a half open door made of stone and from there we walk through a narrow corridor to an amphitheatre. A capsule like an egg made from glass lies in the middle and inside is Neil, asking us to get him out; we can't hear his voice, but it is obvious from all his ridiculous pantomime. I feel like laughing and I smile without caring if he notices or not. He makes a rude gesture.

Me: I do not wish to help him. He deserves to be like a hen in his egg.

Steve: Please Troy, he doesn't deserve that. He didn't leave you behind when you couldn't walk. Remember? He might act a little aggressively from time to time, but he helped us and, even if we don't like him that much, he is our fellow.

Me: Ok.

Steve is always right. Steve never gets upset. Steve has self-control; or shall I call it shallow emotions? Anyway, whatever.

Me: How exactly did he get in? I suppose the same way he can get out.

Steve: That's the mystery. I don't know.

Me: But he must know.

Steve: Let's ask him.

We are trying to ask him by shouting our words, then repeating them slowly, writing the letters on the air with our fingers, gesturing all over the place with hands and feet. He nods and waves his hand like he is not sure. Something like in a movie trailer and the movie has frozen to a frame, and the frame is him. Him encapsulated. An instant thought comes to my mind; my dream. Do I create it? By dreaming I cause a reality? Or better; by dreaming I cause somebody else's hallucination? Because, I mean, it is difficult to accept all this as reality. Movie, game, drug, but not a reality. My thought producing time segmentation? Frames? Let's rephrase it. My own mind projected?

Me: There's nothing we can do; he will soon be out. He has to relax and wait.

At the same time, I decide to speak to Steve about my dream.

Steve: So, we are in the movies and he didn't set the program up well.

Me: Yes.

Steve: I can't remember. Of course, it sounds more reasonable than anything else. The maze, the infection. Didn't make sense. This sounds, how can I say, realistic, pragmatic. Only I can't remember anything. Is it only your thought programmed to be projected? Is every thought of yours projected? Is it?

Me: One question at a time. I don't know. It depends, I suppose, what the idiot has set up as an initial stage. We are three of us; we come with quite a lot of possibilities or patterns. Let's wait to smash his egg and then we can ask him.

Steve: The important question is how long we are going to be trapped.

Me: Yes, that's true.

Steve: But if we are in the movies, we paid for some amount of time, right?

Me: Maybe, or we credited our accounts.

I doubt my own answer.

Steve: Yes, but they must have a limit of use.

Me: Maybe, but possibly we have set it before using their technology or ...

Steve: Or?

Me: Someone will look for us; we must have parents or brothers or something.

Steve: I don't remember.

I am right. Neil is next to us for a while, but he seems strange.

Neil: Come on. The sea is near; let's see the place.

He remembers nothing about his egg capsule.

Neil: Stupidity is contagious.

Steve raises his shoulders.

Steve: Ok at least he is out.

Neil: I am bored with both of you. I am cursed to wander around with two morons.

We don't answer.

Steve to Me: We have to think about your thought projections. It is perhaps the key to get out of this movie, game, whatever it is.

Hierophile: Initiation

For my first gathering, the seven priests carried their seven identifications. Spade, Sword, Rod, Sickle, Lightning Bolt, Star, and Caduceus. Three of them, wearing veils, were dressed in long crimson robes, and another three in helmet, lance and breast plate. One of them, the bearer of Caduceus, had a diadem made from gold and a ruby ring on his small finger. He was naked, keeping only a whip at his waist. I haven't seen Menath.

'Dear Daughter of the Moon, the time of maturity came; we have seven questions, you have only one answer.' *The man in the Diadem was speaking with a beautiful, strong voice. This voice had a soft trembling, like a sparrow's flight over my head, and at the same time a heavy accent, like a monsoon over the bitter lakes. I felt thrilled but without fear. Six girls and six boys came in dressed in long white robes. I was in the middle of the circle. The girls moved to the centre, raised a white sheet, took off my robe and dressed me with a new black dress.*

Then, they moved back and made two rows, each row by three girls and three boys; I was on the top, where the two rows were intersecting like a fleet of birds ready to fly. Bells rung and the sistrum played as ten more priests in veils came in, nine holding torches in their hands and one a silver plate. The Man with the Caduceus said to them, 'welcome my daughter to her initiation.'

Petals flew all over and a fire was set in one of the twin altars in the middle of the chamber. The smoke had a beautiful strong smell. The Man came near the fire. He said, 'Where are you?'

'Night,' *I replied.* 'All things are called?'

'Fiery.'

'Will you gird?'

'Death.'

'Has been wrapped?'

'Serpent.'

'Who is the Father?'

'Leon.'

'Did you become?'

'By him.'

'He will say?'

'Drink.' *Then he came closer, almost face to face and said,* 'there is no way to tell where the self ends, and the world begins. May this be your secret. Immortality.'

The smoke was now heavy and the smell even stronger; the three men in crimson veils moved in front of me, one by one. They offered me drink and nourishment. The first man, a black, strong tasting, thin leaf; the second man, a small piece of greenish bread; and the third man, a yellow, sweet liqueur. The Man stared at me. I felt the urgency to speak, 'nine bows are moving, keep them tight in the Nile's mouth.'
The Man replied, 'we will do as you command.'

'When the moon is at his natal position, unconquerable is the Sun,' *I said.*

The Man, in great voice announced, 'the Oracle has spoken. Let us now drink. The Oracle has spoken. Let us now eat.'

The three men in breast plates shared the rest of the leaf, bread and liquid among the ten veiled priests. The Man said, 'May all of you be blessed.'
They all bent their knees in front of him. The Bull was white, walked slowly, guided by a string held by two men. It looked dizzy and without strength, its blood pouring furiously from the vein in his neck. The animal did not spasm or show any sign of aggressiveness. Was quiet in a fatal acceptance of death. The naked Man approached with his right leg constraining the Bull's hoof and left leg bent as if resting on the Bull's back. He said in his velvet voice, 'come here Daughter of the Moon.'

I walked. Three corns of wheat were bonded at the Bull's tail; a boy was holding a silver cup under his wound, catching the blood that was now streaming all over the floor. A Snake moved on the floor near my feet.

'Drink now,' *the soft voice asked me. I took the silver cup and I left it near the altar, then I touched the animal's flesh with my lips and drank from the wound. My action caused murmuring and some dazedness in the crowd, but the naked man seemed not to mind; instead he seemed satisfied. He raised the cup and gave it to the man with the rod. He drank. The cup moved from hand to hand, to all the six priests carrying the identifications and then to the ten veiled men. The twelve young boys and girls left the ceremony, carrying only the white sheet now stained red by the blood of the Bull. The Snake was around my body. The Bull was slowly passing out, quiet like a thin breeze over the night. I touched the chest of the Man; the Snake moved over the Bull, like a crown on the animal's head.*

The crowd stopped frozen; no sound escaped them, and then the sistrum started and bells followed; the sistrum played faster, when the thunder fell. The man with the Rod came closer; I took a step back. The two men with the Sword and the Sickle walked quickly over to me and kept my hands tight behind my back. The man with the Spade, took off my dress. The man with the Star bent in front of me and said, 'have no fear.'

The nine veiled priests made a circle around the altar that wasn't used until now. The Bull lay still. The man with the rod asked me to enter the circle. We walked, the four of us. But I entered the circle alone while the six identification priests made a half circle around the Bull. I stayed still in front of the altar. I saw the six priests cutting the head of the Bull, then opening the animal and taking out his heart. The veiled priest with the silver plate came near them. The heart, a pinkish red, lay now on the silver disk. The priest walked towards me, entered the circle and gave me the disk.

'Feed him the bull's heart, feed him and pray.'

The six priests were there, eating the raw parts from the Bull's intestines. Six wolves tearing their prey into pieces. The Man walked towards me; I left the disk on the altar. With a fast movement I took the whip he carried at his waist and I hit the air on the top of his head with force; then I tried to whip his face. His hand was on mine. He took back the whip; he looked angry and ready to crash it on my body.

'I am the Serpent's daughter,' *I said*. 'Nobody touches me.'

The Serpent moved from the Bull onto my head, mounting a morbid crown. The naked man left the whip to drop.

'I am the Serpent,' *he said*. 'Feed me now.'

The walls fell apart; the strong pillars lost their density. Millions of tiny peculiar spheres broke, like sudden hailstones. We were alone.

'I am your crown,' *he said*, 'Feed me now.'

We were alone in black waters.

'I am the Bull,' *he said*. 'Feed me now.'

We were alone in red waters.

'I am your child,' *he said*. 'Feed me now.'

We were alone in a dream. A razor wind took my breath, the storm bursting inside my body. The heart of the Bull was beating in the Man's mouth. With my teeth, I cut a piece and I ate it fast.

'How you dare,' *he said*, 'to bite shamelessly my heart?'

'I love you,' *I said*. 'I must possess you.'

He smiled.

'That is impossible,' *he said*.

'That is possible,' *I insisted in fervour.*

The nine veiled priests kissed my hand and left; the priest with the silver plate said, 'the wolves are gone, his wolves are gone. Dear Hierophile, you are the waving star.'

He kissed my Omphalos.

'Sibyl is now your name. Impregnate affinity and immortality alike. Impregnate the cruel beauty.'

'I am not a Sibyl,' *I said.* 'I impregnate only the man, not the child.'

'Dear Daughter of the Moon, may your wish come true,' *the priest replied.*

Hierophile: Delos

I walked out. It was a steel night. The sea was shivering beautifully under the moon's light. I was swimming slowly, going deeper and deeper. I looked back. The moon had a yellowish colour; gigantic palm trees were moving their boughs like fingers, waving to me, asking me to return. I tried, but my feet wouldn't obey my will. I tried, but I was heavy, ready to sink like a stone into the depths of the silverfish waters. Too far from land, too far from Heliopolis. The bog; I thought I was near the bog, the quagmire. A boat was floating slowly onto the black waters. I noticed the shadow of a light and the men's wooden blades as they struck the mouldy waters in the quietness of the night. Had they seen me? I couldn't say. I tried to scream but my voice was lost in my mouth, unable to reach their ears. The light came closer. My necklace, reflecting the moon, was made of precious lapis lazuli, dressed in silver and glass.

Someone saw the spark, noise came from the boat, a man threw himself into the water.

First Man: A mermaid. Eiii here she is, a mermaid and she is alive.

The boat came closer.

Second Man: No, she is a woman and she is fucking gorgeous; she can get a good price in Delos.

They all agreed. I couldn't speak. Someone gave me a little water and a blanket. The sea people. I was a prisoner.

Second Man: Let's take her to the ship.

They turned back and moved towards the bog, or what I thought was the bog. An old ship lay in the dark sea, like a lazy dog in the middle of a dark street. The crew gathered around me. No one dared to approach. I was wearing the sign of the Bull. They knew. All knew.

Third Man: You never touch a woman wearing the sign; you die the most horrible of all deaths, the snake's revenge.

They stayed silent.

Third man: Nasty gift you brought, Anisidor. Nasty omen. Better just to leave; let's leave and we will sell her to Delos; she can get a good price there. All of you stay away as far you possibly can. Do not touch even a hair of her head. Leave her alone. *He spoke loudly, irritated, with a dreadful voice while the fear was shaking her tune's vibration to a foaming climax; the sound of broken paddles in the sea's misfortunes. I slept, the dark wine waters were tranquil, the moon beautifully warm, almost tender. I felt a hand touching me, touching my backbone, I opened my eyes. Anisidor was near, looking at me with admiration and fear.*

Anisidor: I am sorry. I didn't mean to wake you up.

The sun was rising; a pink beam fell on my necklace, reflecting the whole sky; Anisidor moved back. He touched his eyes with fear.

Anisidor: I can't see. I can't see.

He screamed painfully. The man of the night came furiously close to him.

Third Man: Stupid con; I told you do not touch her.

Hierophile: It's okay.

I stood up walked to Anisidor and touched his eyes. Anisidor fell on his knees.

Anisidor: My goddess. I am at your order, a slave.

Hierophile: Bring me water.

He rushed.

Hierophile: I am thirsty.

Nobody moved or said anything. The whole crew was shaking from fear. I was walking naked in front of a crew hungry for women, with Anisidor next to me as a faithful dog.

Hierophile: Delos. We go to Delos.

It took us three days and nights. The mariners felt relief when I stepped on the land. Anisidor followed me. He bought me a linen white dress and we went to the market. I ate honey, bread and an orange. Anisidor ate the same. People stared at us. Anisidor carried a sword made from silver at his waist. We went to the temple. The Lion's head, marble painted blue and gold. The priest came out. He bent.

Priest: Hierophile, welcome to your home.

Anisidor waited outside.

Priest: We were expecting you.

Hierophile: I know.

Priest: Of course, you know.

I noticed a small pyramid near the altar, constructed of painted wooden squares, some black, some white, keeping intact the ratio of an equilateral triangle.

Hierophile: You count then towards the new millennium?

Priest: Yes, my lady. But there are so many. You can never tell who is going to live and who is going to die.

Hierophile: Menath knows, I suppose.

Priest: No, no, him neither. No one can tell; it is a new branch. They come like fallen stars, one in each century, but not for long; they will increase in numbers like hail falling in a spring storm.

Hierophile: I remember; I have seen it.

Priest: Does Anisidor know?

Hierophile: No, no yet.

Priest: He needs time.

Hierophile: Not only. He needs to make an effort. He can understand only what he has.

Priest: The trophy then.

Hierophile: Possibly.

Priest: Or perhaps the hunting.

Hierophile: Great idea.

Priest: Give him his destiny.

Hierophile: I will.

Priest: They always believe that they are the hunters.

Hierophile: Yes, they do.

Priest: Poor little flies.

Hierophile: Do not feel sorry for them; they deserve the big black spider.

Priest: Yes, but still I cannot avoid feeling sorry.

Hierophile: The male bond?

Priest: You can see it this way, but you know well, my dear, I am a eunuch. My name is Lily.

I walked to the altar.

Lily: My dear oracle, Hierophile. Here is your throne.

Two priests wearing the masks of the Bull and the Lion came in. Then a young girl, naked, holding a bowl of water and a sea sponge in her hands, approached the altar. A Tetras was formed. The young girl touched me with the sponge. Fine, perfumed by flowers; water, falling drop by drop at my back bone. The priest with the Bull's mask on his face walked to the altar. The girl was pretty; thin pale face, emerald eyes, yellowish hair. The priest with the Lion's mask on his face walked to the altar.

'Kill her,' *I said.*

The Bull took a knife. Lily had her hands tied. The Lion closed her mouth.

'Now,' *I said.*

A tear fell on my hands; the blood from her veins spread all over me. The Bull fell into a frantic delirium; a loud roar came out of his chest; the Lion was leaking her blood; Lily was staring at me. A scorpion moved on the ground. I felt his sting on my ankle; the pain was sweet, moving heat through my bones to my neck, creating a delirious craving.

Hierophile: *Kymvala pepwka.*

Lily: May gods bless you.

Hierophile: Love is a crime.

Lily: Sinned forever.

Hierophile: Her name is Drusiana; she will live. We killed only her icon. Anisidor needs a wife.

Lily: Sweet criminal, you give her a birth.

Hierophile: Yes, I will give her a birth. Death is not her destiny. Anisidor will be her husband.

Lily: May all be happy for an eternity.

The pale body of the girl was naked, in full beauty.

Hierophile: Bring flowers and perfumes. Let Anisidor reach the altar.

Anisidor came in looking around suspiciously. His eyes stopped on Drusiana's bloodless body.

Hierophile: Look at her. She is sleeping but she will wake up if you desire her.

Lily spread a strong fragrance using a round cup with small holes on its surface and fired up all the thyrsus in the main hall. The odour was heavy.

Hierophile: Do you desire her? Do you wish her as your wife?

Anisidor nodded yes and his eyes darkened; a storm was passing fast from his forehead. Revenge. I saw revenge, hatred and passion all in one gaze.

Hierophile: Do not get frustrated, my dear friend. We only killed her icon, not the girl.

Drusiana opened her eyes.

Hierophile: The lunar animal illuminates the celestial fields. On the palm of my hands have I graven thee? She is a venerable goddess. Your share of happiness attends you. Raise up her heart. Excellence may endure. The only child. Fruit bearer. Within her a root. Within her the foundations of Atum.

I declared in an affirmative voice. The mysterious envelop carried both eloquence and muteness, both affirmation and suggestion. The girl stood up and walked out of the temple. Her hair had a reddish glint. Anisidor seemed uncertain.

Hierophile: She is not real, an icon only.

I repeated while Anisidor stayed silent.

Anisidor: But you said exactly the opposite, that you killed only an icon.

He spoke helplessly at last.

Hierophile: You have to win your path. You have to win her.

Anisidor: I don't know how. Could you help me?'

His words had the sound of regret.

Hierophile: Yes, I will. But you have to run the whole way by yourself. I guide only the worthy ones. Move now. Make your own destiny.

Anisidor walked out of the temple.

Lily: Roots spring from the seed. Pleasure and pain shall complete the day. Gifts are never free.

Hierophile: Lily, when will Heliodromus rise?

Lily: The sun's Rider, my dear, lies now in the rock. The arrow shot, awaiting the sun's Archer.

Hierophile: We must fire the bolt for the Chariot.

Lily: Precession of equinoxes?

Hierophile: The cosmic motion, shifting the spheres.

Lily: The constellation of Perseus.

Hierophile: Not yet. Gorgon is still alive. The cavern is governed by her.

Lily: Tauroctony needs baptism.

Hierophile: Mark the forehead and move then.

Lily: Do not rush, my lady. She has the power to annihilate time.

Hierophile: The Traveller?

Lily: The Traveller has the Shepherd's crook. We wait for him. The Water Brooks. It will last an instant. Then you must fall into the Lacuna; the Gorgon gives the egg birth, and she flings four wings.

Hierophile: I see. The keys then must be two. One for the Corax and one for the Pater.

Lily: Yes. That's it. The raven and his master.

Hierophile: The fighting Eagle is his own incarnation?

Lily: You can see it this way. But he is not incarnated; the flesh passes through the cavern, his spirit prey to continual error.

Hierophile: The Mother then?

Lily: The Mother? Felix and Magus.

Hierophile: The City of Gathering?

Lily: All end up in Omphalos.

Hierophile: The homonym is only derived from the motion.

Lily: I am not sure. Aeons are crossing lines of the world to come.

Hierophile: But it is not a living world.

Lily: Unfortunately.

Hierophile: The folly.

Lily: It is him; she has no alternative.

Hierophile: She will kill him?

Lily: I think so.

Hierophile: But then she is obliged to kill herself and that is impossible.

Lily: No. It is possible.

Hierophile: How? She is immortal.

Lily: To us. Not to her.

Hierophile: But it is a constant resurrection; she will have to rise.

Lily: She found the exit. She will end everything.

Hierophile: No, no, it is not fair.

Lily: You cannot stop it, Hierophile.

Hierophile: I will.

Lily: How? With Anisidor? It is too early.

Hierophile: I know, but the breath flashes fast. We have to be prepared.

Lily: Mother loves you, but she loves him more. She will not choose.

Hierophile: She will choose. Her life falls on me. I am living her life.

Lily: You think that you live her life. Illusion is the first step to folly. You will simply lose yourself.

Hierophile: But I have aid. My sister.

Lily: Your sister will die soon out of love for the golden god. She feeds her with poisonous milk. Love destroys the oracle's powers.

Hierophile: No. She will not die.

Lily: Maybe, you never know.

Hierophile: I want to be alone for a while.

Lily: Feed the pyramid then. The squares must change rule, then you might have a chance.

> *The pyramid. The fatal astro, reversed like a fallen meteorite. Square by square diving into the sky. Diving into the galactic ashes, diving without fear, waving, waiting, dreaming? For what? A home? A dome? A dog-star? The hunter was there; waiting. His dog barking, chasing the souls, grabbing them in their teeth, carrying them like a flock of birds to his master. They did not know; poor trembling souls*

prepared for such a horrific destiny. Poor little sparks of light ready to be swollen like small insects from the bird's mouth.

'Horus,' *I begged.* 'My master and son; Horus. Help me. I must change the rule; time is pressing; it is reversing fast; my days are now in a constant run. Horus, child of my womb, child of my future birth, help me.'

His mind is a frozen fire. He lied; he was unable to love; his love was a hunting game, a cell, a number in his rules. He was not the Snake. He was the Bull. The Mother let him. She has let him free. She is afraid of me. She let him free to gain my virginity, to dissolve my power.

'Why, Mother? Why? Horus, we have to kill him before he gets to us.'

The pyramid stood there.

'How can I change the rule?'

A rainbow shaft brighter than any other: The spindle of necessity, the path of sky, the plane of oblivion, the river of Lethe. All ended in divine madness. The rule was unchanged. I counted the time; the pyramid was stable for a while, and I knew for a moment that I had only to move one square and push the next into the first's place; this move would gain us some time. My hands pushed the black square and moved the white. The rule changed. The repetitive pattern gave four more Spirals before the end of the branch. Then I moved backwards from white to black. Sum eight times.

'What if I release one?'

I had an overflow that leads to accumulation. I wished Mnemon, my brilliant colleague in the Menath's school, was here. He could have done it far better. He would have found a way to earn more time.

'Mnemon,' *I spoke to myself,* 'We have to find him and bring him to the last supper. It is our only chance.' *Lily came in.*

Lily: Oh, not bad at all.

Hierophile: Mnemon would have done it better.

Lily: Yes, for sure. But the pyramid obeys only to the right hands.

Hierophile: We need him or an advisor. Someone better than me. We need aid. I was never brilliant in fitting the patterns; they are so confusing when they form their spiralling clusters.

Lily: Pretty well, my Hierophile. I have to congratulate your effort.

Hierophile: It was the simplest solution. I had no better idea.

Lily: It works though.

Hierophile: It seems for a while. Where is Drusiana?

Lily: She is dreaming. Rising from the dead, without drink from the spring; it is such a painful dream. She cannot remember, neither has she forgot. Half of her wishes to breathe and the other half wishes to stop breathing.
Hierophile: Bring her to me. We must walk together for a while. Delos is too dry for her. We need to pass to the Forest of the Unknown.

Troy: The Sun's Chariot

The voice of Steve reaches my ears absorbed as I am in my own thoughts.
Steve: Troy, look, the altar.
Me: Yes, I see.
We walk towards a marble construction, hanging like a heavens star in the middle of a circle, made by a granite spread with greenish veins and crimson waves.
Neil: What an unbelievable beauty.
Neil is on his knees looking at the basement's designs.
Neil: Guys, he is the Bull. I remember his sign from the school years.
Me: Yes. Mithras.
Neil: I thought that it is an Egyptian temple.
Steve: It might be some sort of sect mixing the Egyptian bull with the Mesopotamian bull.
Me: Maybe.

Steve touches the sculptured god then his own cheek and passes his hand through his hair. His hair now has a reddish glint. Neil and I look at him, thrilled. A drop of blood has fallen from his nose onto the floor. Steve, standing in full allure, a prince covered by the aura of an alien myth. Covered by clouds of fire, the breath of space, the space's waving sea. Currents flow from the top and sides of the temple, lights of fruited vines. Fine-looking like he has never been before, his body a bow, the Archer. His body impresses upon the raised chord. An arrow and a bow at the same time.

Neil touches the altar impatiently, then his own cheeks and head; he takes off his clothes and touches all his body like he is taking a shower. Does he wish his own metamorphosis? I stand astonished, looking as those two men are transformed into the sun's charioteers, the Archer and the Rider. Suddenly Steve turns into a pale white figure and Neil is growing dark, almost black. Two wild horses running into a false sky. I am all alone.

'Oh my gosh,' *I say aloud to myself*. 'Is it Er? The four openings? Are we dead? We were soldiers once. Maybe we are just three dead soldiers, running their destiny into the underworld.'

The altar moves; a girl with a face like the shadow of the moon looks at me. Her face is a dying cloud, only eyes, nothing else, eyes; floating eyes, shaded thunders, grasping my breath, getting my soul.

'Do not love,' *she said.*

'I loved once,' *she said.*

'Do not love me. Do not betray me. Love me. Then I may have the chance to betray you,' *she said.*

'He was called once, Anisidor. I was called once, a girl. The Bull took her heart. The Lion gave her a forged love. The Snake was her only destiny. She knew; she knew from the beginning she couldn't possess, only be possessed, but she tried; she tried hard to save your world. To save you, Troy, to save you. Do not drink; do not wash, only swim. Fall and swim into the darkness; the bog ship is waiting; reach me at Delos. Troy, hurry up. Reach me at Delos. We move to the Forest of the Unknown. She is taking me there where the Oracle cannot see. Where she has no chance other than me, the drowned daughter of her blood. Troy, he is going to eat her heart; she took her to a forest, a raining forest, just to drop her alone, to leave her without a heart. He is working against her; he is working the rock and the bow. She is strong but now weak, weak from love. Oracles are not allowed to love. In love they submit; they become common voiceless women. But she is in deep love, fighting all alone. Troy help her; she is helping you. Time is not real. Just a dimension. Cross the threshold, move and hold her. Make her see. He is a liar, a false god. A liar, a stealer. He is stealing from her, and then he smiles without her memory. Help her. His heart will change; his heart will be hers for all coming centuries. The Snake waits, waits for us all. The crowning Snake prepares the Omphalos where all the emanations even the Bull's heart will be eaten piece by piece; the machine is gearing, speeding; be ready, Troy. Get out, fall fast into the water, keep Steve and Neil close to you. Keep them. They are your companions, your only companions. Find fast the Holy Island, and then the Bull's forest. Help her. Help her and win me.'

My two friends are there almost without breath, ghost like, unable to think themselves.

Me, to Neil and Steve: Walk after me; quicken your pace. Run with me.

The misty sea is trembling like the girl's voice. The moon has a yellowish colour; gigantic palm trees are moving their boughs like fingers, waving to me, asking me to follow the sea's stream.

Me, to Neil and Steve: Move. Fast.

I throw myself into the waters; my two friends have done the same. The moon shivering the sea's waves, a silver path. We are going to die, if we are not already dead. Then I hear the blades. The ship. Half-naked men. We are in their ship. Three ghosts in a bog ship.

Me: Who is the captain?

Anisidor: I am.

The voice comes as the sound of an empty cave, the sound of a broken wood in the twilight of an ancient sky. The man holds a silver sword.

Anisidor: I am your guide to Delos. Follow my instructions; three days trip and then you landed.

Me: Your name please?

Anisidor: It once was Anisidor; now it is forgotten.

Me: Forgotten by whom?

Anisidor: By her, by me, by the moon. Forgotten.

Me: Why?

Anisidor: She got trapped in the forest. He gave her to drink, the potion of Lethe. He lied to her. She thought him a friend, but he was an enemy. The Bull wanted her lost. He tricked her, played with her, fooled her. He wanted only her thoughts. Stealing thoughts and emotions. A common stealer. A thief.

Me: Drusiana?

Anisidor: No, Hierophile. Drusiana has no voice; she is an icon, drowned icon, following her like a shadow. She followed her hoping for real life, but the forest was made by paper and colour; no real life there. Only the barking of distant dogs, only the waters cracking from the cement. The buildings were prisons of fire. The arrows poisonous, fell on her body like an iron rain. I tried running after her, but she had no eyes, no ears, only desire. Her passion. For a moment, we heard a whisper; her sister called her name; she said to her: my dear Hierophile, be careful; he will steal your power; be careful, run, run, run away. Get Anisidor's sword, kill him, and then decapitate the Bull; he is just a lie, their way to get the best of us. Destroying our purity with their slaughter machine. Come back, ask Anisidor to help you. Anisidor, her sister told me, run after them, get Drusiana; hold her tight to your body until she stops breathing, then kiss her and give her your strength; she will lead Hierophile to her destiny. I ran and did as I was told, but the Hunter was there. He gazed at me. Then he threw the thunder and burned my flesh, turning me to a shadow. I had no chance; Hierophile stood without moving her lips, without moving her hands; if she only said my name, it would have been enough.

Me: The Snake?

Anisidor: The Snake abandoned her; she cares only for Omphalos and her son.
Me: What about me?
Anisidor: A last chance. She moved you some time ago, knowing the trap was awaiting her. You are our last chance. Hurry up. Get her out of this horror. Then we will move all together. The West is falling, the East is vanishing; move to the Ponte. The dark waters. There is the Fleece. We get the seal and we move until we reverse the pyramid. Steve knows how to reverse the game; he was called Mnemon once, centuries ago, the chariot's Archer. It will all come to him once he finds himself in front of the console. Neil, do not underestimate Neil; he runs fast when future calls the second Spiral; Tiras is his real name and he was our best chariot's rider; he can get Heliodromus and shift the orbits. The Mehen has six Emanations and four Spirals; we are in the first Spiral. We have no time, Troy.

Hierophile: Methexis

The forest is dark, no light; boughs and grey branches keep the sky imprisoned. Drusiana walks near me, pale like a hiding star. I see him, sitting underneath an olive tree. Olive trees do not exist in the Forest of the Unknown. I know it isn't a real tree; it is him envisioning a tree.
Mithras: From the North to call Decrepit Winter, from the South to bring Solstitial summer's heat.
Hierophile: What are the roots that clutch, what branches grow?
Mithras: Oh Hierophile, you are such a child. Remember me, don't you? Your memory picks all she could find to build a tower from glass. You intend to imprison me here, don't you? Seeking, as you do, the right word, simply to beguile the Merlin. When was your first time? I think I remember; the aery port sheltering the warmth of North. Of course, since then the idea has fallen in your head. Then you painted with words. Spells. Your words are spells. And you thought that Proclus dreamed you back there, so many centuries ago, when he said theurgy is possible only through henads. Tethys is the name of fountain; the fontal fluxions are celebrating after the Saturnian monad in the kingdom of Rhea. The fire Sermon. Then you remembered your Cumean sister, the Jar's muse. Poor Hierophile, is your existence true or a lie of your Mother? Did you ever wonder that you might not have any of your qualities and all you thought was yours is just her dream, her poisonous dream, her little escaping moment? Did you ever think that you may be worth nothing more than any piece of paper onto which someone has quoted thoughts and words of so many others? Do you hear, Hierophile?

Others. Nothing is yours, a reference; or can I say, an appendix to the books you read? Your spells have no value, are not powerful, are dramatic; yes, so dramatic exactly because you believed them; you took them as parts of your psyche. Power? You have none. Prediction? You are unable to foresee even the rain that is ready to fall on our heads. Poor Hierophile, you are just a dream, someone else's dream.

He seems irritated. He stands up wrathfully.

Mithras: Why do you carry her around? She died a long time ago. You killed her, as I have been told. Why? To play the future god? Now you try to give her life. You call this resurrection? Your silly understanding of metaphysics. Do you really think that anybody is interested in her shadow? You look pathetic. Approach little fool. I am your only hope. Your last hope. Drink from the sky fountain. The cause of division is called *methexis.*

Drusiana looks at me terrified. But I can't resist; I can't. I drink from Mithras' hands. I turn my head to the sky; the Raven and the Eagle are fighting. He holds my hand and looks at my eyes. Then he grasps Drusiana by the hand and kisses her. I close my eyes. The rain is falling, dripping into my soul. Humidity is Death or Eros, or so I remember Menath saying one day. Am I dying? I am here alone. Drusiana is so thin of a shadow, losing all her strength after his kiss.

Horus: Poor daughter of the lost souls, he is not interested in you; curiosity was driving him. He wanted to see the strange creature of the spiralling pools. He wanted to taste an earthy soul and dive his fingers into your hair.

Horus: Σιβυλλα τι θελεις;

Hierophile: The thunder.

Horus: And the sword?

Hierophile: You see her?

Horus: She will soon die.

Hierophile: No. Nothing has been lost. Look. The Snake.

'Get him,' I say. 'Mother, get him.' The Snake glares for a moment at Mithras' eyes then slips away. I walk to Drusiana. Our bodies, our arms, two thrown in earth beams of purple rooting into a vegetative form, mixed with each other in the same essence of green. Time has no importance in the Forest. You cannot count, you cannot count, you cannot count.

Troy: The Forest of the Unknown

Me: What is this dry rock?

Anisidor: Delos, Troy.

It seems a derelict landscape. Anisidor says that Delos vanished after Hierophile was gone. The island became that dry rock. Lily, her priest, is a stele with few letters of no meaning.

Me: Let's see.

The sun is bright; my two brothers are now walking fast behind us.

Anisidor: Here it is. Lily. The stele of Delos.

Anisidor points at a broken marble. A small flower is trying to find a drop of water underneath the stele. Steve touches his petals; a tear falls from his eyes to the flower's root; suddenly we are in the Forest. The four of us. Walking our way. Steve is strong as an enormous mountain. Neil is winged as a fired storm. Anisidor opens our way with his silver sword.

Steve: The tree. Do we have to climb? Troy, do we have to climb?

Me: I think so. Here it is only the anus; we need the mouth. The tree is a fucking tube; watch, watch your steps. The giants are only the gears; the fear is the mouth, digesting all that is flesh.

Anisidor: I am not; none of us is. We are thoughts; her thoughts. Thus, we can move. *We climb like sailors to their ship. The night falls unevenly, at once, like a veil. Time for rest. The Sun will move us again tomorrow.*

Hierophile: I was not; I was; I am not; I do not care; Ει καλως ειρηται το λαθε βιωσας.

Me: Who said that?

Steve: No one. The tree whistles from time to time.

Neil: Shall we elevate?

Me: I will go first.

Anisidor: We must turn from South to East.

Me: Where is she?

Steve: It seems empty.

Anisidor: She wishes death.

Me: For how long?

Anisidor: I think, since she gave Drusiana a drop of her blood.

Me: Why has she done that?

Anisidor: It is the pyramid. She tried to apply the infinitesimal into the integral.

Me: And?

Anisidor: And she found that it does not work.

Steve: Leibniz was wrong after all.

Neil: Are all of you insane?

Steve: But Pascal said it is all about justice.

Me: She misunderstood.

Anisidor: Human error.

Me: Look how it works. From South to East with respect to the factor. Make the factor less than 1 and 1⁄2 and 1⁄3 and 1⁄5 and the same. Then move the square, decreasing the rule according to the spaces left and finally rotate 90 degrees each of them.

Steve: Oh no, it is madness; it does not work this way. Recalculate.

Me: Multiply speed by time; you will get the distance.

Steve: But we do not know the speed, as we do not know the time.

Me: No, we can just bind it as a utility tool.

Steve: Does it function?

Me: If you get the horizontal axis and project it to the vertical. Then the curve shadows the reflection.

Steve: Unstable. We search equilibria.

Anisidor: *Ceteris paribus.*

Neil: Enough. Keep your mouths shut. You speak nonsense.

Hierophile: Fission. Two people at a time, continuous with one another. Recursive functionals. Every property belongs to one. The realm of *salva veritate*. The present is a part of the past, or maybe it is the future that holds past? My certainty drives me to say the second. The future holds us all.

Me: Do you see her? Steve, where is Neil?

Steve: He walked too fast; he is injured. Anisidor stayed with him.

Me: Which one must we rescue, her or Drusiana?

Steve: I am not sure.

Me: We must answer this question before we move further. We cannot save both; they will become released as conflict, causing mental disturbance.

Steve: Do we really have to decide?

Me: Maybe not.

Steve: What if we just move without them?

Me: We can't. We are in the first Spiral. She has the Spindle. We save her. Drusiana is accidental. An assumption, her sublimation. We go for her. Let the shadow spring the tree. Let the gods decide.

Troy: Save her and run

Steve takes a deep breath. The tree has a rotten smell. I feel nauseous.

Steve: Do you see them, Troy?

Me: Yes, I am close.

Steve: Is a storm coming? The water will cover the whole area.

Me: I know. It is mud water, from a rotten sky.

Steve: Here she is.

Me: Drusiana?

Steve: Yes.

We are near. She is a thin little girl.

Steve: She is very young, maybe eight or nine years old. I thought that she was older.

Me: Time runs backwards for her.

Steve: What do we do? I can't leave a child to die.

Me: All right then. Take her out of here.

Steve: I will.

Steve takes her in his arms and moves to the roots. I have to go on.

Me: Stay with Anisidor and Neil; try to move them out. The construction seems unstable.

Steve: Yes, I intend to do exactly that.

I walk alone. The tree is not a tree. The branches are coming out of deserted earth. The sky has the colour of a greyish mouse. There she stands. I come closer. She has blizzard eyes.

Hierophile: Troy, is that you?

Me: Yes.

Hierophile: Too late.

Me: No, we have time; it is only the first Spiral.

Hierophile: The *Tetractys* is still folding. Do you see him?

Me: No. I see only you.

Hierophile: Look carefully.

Then I see.

Me: He is inside you.

Hierophile: He is taking form.

Me: Who is he?

Hierophile: Horus. His birth might be my death.

Me: We have Drusiana.

Hierophile: I know. Keep her safe. She might have a chance.

Me: What are you going to do?

Hierophile: Give birth to him and let him decide. And you?

Me: We move to Ponte.

Hierophile: Wise decision. Then move West.

Me: Why West?

Hierophile: He said that the Centre has moved, and Thebes is now in the new regiment. He must go there to refund his lands. The pawns of creation.

Me: The Snake?

Hierophile: She is happy; her son is coming to life. She has her second chance.

Me: And you?

Hierophile: I do not know. I dream that he is my lover.

Me: A vertigo. Son or lover?

Hierophile: I give birth only to love.

Me: Nonsense. You give birth to your fears.

Hierophile: Stop it Troy. That is unfair.

Me: He is insane.

Hierophile: Not really. Only seems so. He will soon be like anybody else.

Me: Like anybody else? What do you mean?

Hierophile: He will have a form; underneath is empty. I will fill him. We are two.

Me: What must we do?

Hierophile: Move to Ponte. Get the Fleece, destroy the halves. Then join us at the second Spiral. Move the pyramid ten times to the left and nine to the right. Add one Square. We all become joined in the World of Mirrors. The city is constructed on the waters, smells like a rotten morass, smells like this tree. There is a clock and a fountain. We meet there.

Me: And him?

Hierophile: Mother will take care of him.

Me: What about Atis?

Hierophile: We will see. The Thundering of Poles. It is not in my memory. Go now. Rush. *I meet the others on the roots. We walk fast.*

Neil: Finally, we saved Drusiana. Nice, quiet girl. What do you think Troy?

Me: Yes. She is really quiet.

Neil: How the hell do we get to Ponte?

Anisidor: We have my ship.

Steve: Do you still think it's correct to interpret our condition as a movie and ourselves as the unwilling actors?

Me: I do not know.

Neil: Either we hallucinate, or we are really there.

Me: Anyway, we must follow the pattern.

Anisidor has the ability to move his ship like a wave in the sea's sound.

Anisidor: Let the night bathe in astral waters boys. We will find the leading star to Ponte.

Me: Our response is a series of observations. We must observe what exists. We must turn the white dwarfs to red dwarfs.

Anisidor: The Big Crunch. Inflation or Ekpyrosis.

Steve: Probably nuclear fusion. The four fundamental interactions.

Me: Please, I don't understand. Ponte is the point of exit?

Steve: Oh no, just the beginning of the second Spiral, exactly as she said.

Me: We must seek the factors. We have to consider the problem.

Neil: Our location is random then?

Steve: No, I do not think so. It is the goal that generates the means.

Neil: You call us means?

Steve: I call us a moment of time. The decision makers.

Neil: To decide about what?

Steve: To define us as the missing dimension. We are constantly referring to time as a linear extension and to space as longitude - latitude of a range extension; we forget to include one more dimension. We search the Infinitum while we occupy it. We are the missing dimension. We can move to Ponte only if we fecundate Ponte.

Me: The world as offspring?

Steve: Exactly. The necessary condition lies within us.

Me: The backgrounds are our landscapes then. We are the creators of the observation.

Steve: We seek because we are able to find. The question carries the answer.

Neil: Immortality then. Our Holy Grail.

Me: We seek immortality, but in what form?

Steve: In the gained control over matter.

Me: Life will spread into all.

Neil: What about Drusiana?

Me: I don't know. She is just a girl. But she is the girl who will give us the Fleece.

Neil: Shall we repeat it all over?

Steve: The mechanics of the Bull. Then the seeds. Then we fight our way out.

Neil: Ready?

Me: We must be.

The ship floats out of the narrow pass; we see the lights of a golden city; a voice is repeating itself like the dream of her gloomy waters. We gather all together and

watch in silence the orange moon, fired with black passion and wild fears, among the city's higher stalagmites. Drusiana approaches, pointing at the sky. A white bird encircling our ship.
Anisidor: The omen! A shy dove over the watery wilderness!
The stern of the ship leaps forward, and a great wave of the surrounding sea surges in her wake.
Steve: We are near.
Neil: What is the name of her ruler?
Anisidor: It is an old name. Medea, the in-between.

Troy: Medea

Modification of weather. The cloud's birth in the atmosphere traverses the suffusion. Triangles of crystalline crossing the projected proximity.
Me: Humans are the embryogenesis of cosmic.
Neil: Who said these nonsenses?
Me: I.
Steve: Troy, you fool. Megalomania arises easily in those lands.
Anisidor: Look. The Grand Steppe. She has lived for centuries now in the same earth. Objects are disengaged from their usual reference. Be careful. The light diffuses. The fog impinges in almost everything. Detachment is the biggest fear. It reflects only her thought.
Medea: I flew out of the circle of the wearisome, heavy grief. I came on with swift feet to the desired crown. I passed beneath the bosom of the Mistress, Queen of the Underworld, 'happy and most blessed one, a god you shall be instead of mortal.' For I also dreamed that I am of your blessed race. But Fate mastered me and then thundered, striking with lighting. A kid fell into milk. Original sin coupled with the innate divinity of mankind. Say to her that Bacchius freed you. A bull, you rushed to milk. Quickly, you rushed to milk. A ram, you fell into milk. The twofold power. The son of beautiful Aether and my tender love.
Neil: She is mad. All this milk drives me sick. I am tired, coping with all these mad females. They give us only spare bits of broken rhymes with no meaning. Are they oracles or just loose minds? Better go back and find a place to live; I mean what a hellish bullshit we are in.
Medea: The Real resists. The Real lacks any possible mediation. Naming brings a new presence. I am the passive voice. You can tie me up if you wish, but there is nothing

more useless than an organ. My mind became a place of refuge, a sanctuary, a room I could enter with no fear of invasion. The Cosmos is moved by ever active sacred lines. I am real, without being actual.

Neil walks towards her furiously.

Neil: There are limitless possibilities of action. You are just an illusion. You are a pen that dreams through other's dreams. A dustbin of words. A deliberate obscurantism. A fiction. Demystification is my purpose. Can you understand that?

Medea: The piercing Eye. Intellect, Reason, Opinion. The genus of poet is divine. Orpheus has four forms: Ram, Bull, Serpent, Lion. The true Serpent is a horned Jove. Pan is the soul of the world. Bacchus has the serpent's head.

Neil: Existence precedes Essence. The object determines the sign. Deduction, Induction or Hypothesis? Here is declared my pragmatism. Prepared to act against the purposeless. Absolute chance. Mechanical necessity. Law of breeding.

Medea: Let me read you a poem. 'I see a lily on the brow. With anguish moist and fever dew.'

Neil: Overturn the Hierarchy at a given moment. Dual oppositions always re-establish themselves. You function on the psychological. You refer not to knowledge, but to disembodied perception. Simply, you try to fool us.

Medea: Close the doors, you, uninitiated.

Neil: There is nothing outside the text that belongs to you.

Medea: Now you have died and now you have come into being.

Neil: I have no fear.

She walks a few steps and gives him the Fleece. We all stand amazed. Neil kisses her hand; then he looks at Drusiana. She approaches. He raises his hands, laying the Fleece on her head and shoulders.

Hierophile: Dreams

I feel bitterness running from my body. My whole existence is emptied, dripping in the earth. I am laying on the ground without me, breathing sharp air that cuts into my heart.

Hierophile: In my dream I was underneath a thorny dome.

Horus: Honeypot ants use their own bodies as living storage. Dreaming laid down the patterns of life.

Hierophile: Do my dreams belong to me?

Horus: Yes, as impressions of your body. You can call them somatoglyphs.

Hierophile: Affections can cause actions?

Horus: Mental images. Immanently mapping the environment.

Hierophile: The Effect created its Cause?

Horus: Neither internal finality nor clearly cut individuality. Image remembrance. You could call it this.

Hierophile: Time or mobility?

Horus: Time and mobility are not progresses, but spatial trajectory.

Hierophile: And you?

Horus: The Spirit-Child. Timeless time of formative creation and perpetual creating.

Hierophile: It rains mud water. Fatigue and dissolution. The smell of annulment.

Horus: Rethink.

Hierophile: Memory is my body's imprint. Word is my living storage. Panopticon is my glass tower. Beguiling me, imprisonment in affection. A sibyl.

Horus: Redefine.

Hierophile: Affection is my dream. Perception is my panopticon. Memory is my conscience. Spelling under my thorny dome.

Horus: No two successive memories are identical, for the one always contains the memory left by the other.

Hierophile: But I am still here not able to move.

Horus: You can run if you wish.

Hierophile: I forgot my wish.

Horus: Then don't.

Horus: And she forgot the stars, the moon, the sun. And she forgot the blue above the trees. And she forgot the dells where waters run. And she forgot the chilly autumn breeze. She had no knowledge when the day was done and the new morn, she saw not.

In my dream the flaming city stirs behind the windows. Shadows of buildings, like clouds of malice, are reaching the sky. The triumph over guilt or the cruelty of the ideal? Plucking at her liver. Penetrating deep into her body.

Hierophile: Bound like clay not yet separated from Earth. Bound with his liver eating Eagle. My sanctuary: the torched moving Guide. My weary dream: the cremate fate of release.

In my dream the city falls. The blank and the motionless has no form. Change and transformation are never at rest. Does Heaven move? Does Earth stand still?

The Eagle answered terrified: 'It can be passed on, but not received. It can be obtained, but not seen. It is rooted in its own self. One order bolted in thy lurk.'

I knew then that the vast sea lies hidden and unseen.

'For the commandment created us free to act lawfully upon the silent deep' *the Eagle said without hesitation.*

Horus: Let man wear the fell of the lion, woman the fleece of the sheep. On what wings dare they aspire? On what immortal hand or eye? From the four Zoas, already one has gone. Move now to the next. Kiss the bride of the dead sire.

Troy: Despair, terror, woe and rage; all of the living chain

We are sitting in the coffee shop near the market. Steve has already had three pints of lager.

Steve: Someday, I am going to change my entire life.

Neil: Of course. After a few more pints everything is possible.

I say nothing. The crowd flows like a river, asking, demanding a chance. Their chance to change their lives.

Steve: It is going from bad to worse. How long is this situation going to persist?

Me: I don't know, maybe six months or a year. And then, the usual, the man of power, the dowry man or whatever.

Steve: They try for self-sustainability.

Neil: Oh yes? Impossible. They fool themselves.

Me: Of course.

Neil: The problem, Troy, is: what we do.

Me: You mean the three of us?

Neil: Yes. We cannot pass all our life drinking horrible beer, of the worse quality, in this coffee place.

Me: We cannot do much.

Steve: We can move to the countryside.

Neil: Where exactly do you live? There is no such thing. Here is safer; the countryside is just an area for plunder and spoiling. Here they feed us for free. There they work without knowing if they will find anything in their farms the next day. Lately, I have seen whole families arriving to find shelter in the city. I asked them. They speak of a sort of plague, menacing the cultivated valleys like an acid rain. They say that it is a slow death.

Steve: And the factory?

Neil: I went there. I walked for two days, lonely like a wolf. I asked them for a job. They told me that they do not need more employees; they have enough. I waited to see, but no one was coming or leaving. It is well known; they hired them in the very beginning; they have special installations inside the factory, no need to move.

Steve: Anyway, we lack petrol; we must be happy that we still have enough food and drink.

Steve strives to reconcile our sadness.

Neil: You call that food? It is just a strange mass of shit.

Steve: But we are fed. And I feel very healthy. The factory provides all.

Neil: How the hell do they provide all? Nothing comes or goes. Nothing at all. No trade, no goods, no materials. What do they do? They shit and then they recycle it to us?

Steve: Oh, come on. You are disgusting Neil. Maybe for the time you were here. You don't know if they just had some arrivals. They use tunnels and electrical trains running from the metro connection near the police station to their station inside the factory.

Neil: Yes, I know, that is how we get our food. But how do they get their supplies? From where, from whom?

Steve: I do not care; I am happy if I can drink or eat.

I decide to change subject; Neil is getting furious and Steve, distressed.

Me: What about your weird neighbour, Steve?

Steve: She is mad. Nowadays she doesn't speak to anyone. A strange noise, like broken gears colliding, comes constantly from her apartment. You know, once I saw her watching the three of us from her window. She left quickly when she saw me staring at her.

Me: Really? Rarely anyone notices her. Anyway, go on, please.

Steve: I went and knocked on her door. She didn't open it. I left her a message. Next day, here she is; come, she said, I must show you something.

Neil: Like what? Her thirsty vine maybe?

Steve: Shut up. She is mad, not a whore.

Neil: You like her?

Steve: No, I just feel sorry for her. I mean she was quite nice in the old days.

Me: And now?

Steve: Simply insane.

Neil: Who is not?

Steve: Yes, but she is bad.

Me: Let him continue.

Steve: She thinks that she has the ability not only to forecast future but to move time.

Neil: Fantastic; does she have a time machine?

Steve: You could say that. She has a wooden box with a key. She has also an iron rod. She told me that this key is for the Pater and there is a second one for the Corax. We have to move to the centre, to Rome, in order to find the second key.

Neil: We?

Steve: Yes. We. She said to me that we are now in the second Spiral. The rod is for you.

Neil: For me?

Steve: Exactly. She also said that we have to see her, and she will arrange for us to move to Rome. Neil will get the rod; those were her exact words. I will get the key.

Me: And I?

Steve: Nothing for you Troy, sorry.

Me: Rome? She said Rome?

Steve: Yes, poor creature, she is getting really bad; I told you already. I tried to say to her that Rome was an ancient city, not existing on any map for centuries now. Of course, there is a village with the name Romm. I asked her if she confuses the village with Rome. She said no. She speaks of The Rome, the centre of the empire. Heliodromus will rise there. We must hurry up. Time is pressing, the second Spiral runs fast. But the third and fourth are speeding in immense acceleration. Mother is moving without care. She lost her interest in us all.

Me: Mother?

Steve: Yes, Mother. I couldn't understand a word.

Me: And how did you reply?

Steve: Something polite; yes, we will be here tomorrow, this kind of stuff, just to get out of her filthy apartment. You know she has a goat? She also has something like a personal garden. I kind of liked it; it was nice. It had a little flower in a corner. She told me that she feeds her goat from her garden and drinks only her milk. I offered to bring her some food if she wished, since I had some spare food vouchers. But she refused. She said that we eat the dead.

Me: The dead?

Steve: Yes, the dead.

Neil: For god's sake, she is right.

Me: Right?

Neil: After I left the factory, my curiosity drove me to the police station metro. There was a train ready to leave; I asked the policeman what he was carrying, he said: the dead. Lately, they move them out of the city to be buried in the countryside, since we lack space here. He said that families have their burial ceremony in a special room in the police building and then, off to the trains. Sad, he said, but convenient. He looked very distressed though. I asked him why he was in such a mood, at least he was lucky enough to have a job. Death rates are constantly increasing. So many people every day, carrying their relatives in the small police car-cabinets, leaving them there like garbage to be carried away. So sad he repeated, so very sad.

Steve: Ok, so what? They have to bury them somewhere.

Neil: It is only one line, you idiot, one single line. One single train that comes and goes. Are both of you cons?

Steve: And you? Are you the smart detective that discovered the truth?

Neil: Fuck you, Steve. We go to see her. Get up. Steve, get up. Let's go. Let's find out what she knows. By the way how old is she?

Steve: I can't say really. She looks old like a grey leaf of autumn, and then she looks kind of sparkling like a spring's ray.

Me: Are you a poet, Steve?

Neil: Ok, ok, enough with your chat. Move your asses and let's see what she knows.

Me: My beer?

Neil: Fuck you and your filthy beer, Troy.

We walk fast, pushing the crowd that moves in the opposite direction toward the main square. A demonstration is on.

Neil: Hell. I am tired of the same spectacle every day.

I couldn't blame him. I think exactly the same. Steve stops. He grabs a man, around his sixties, by his shirt and asks him what exactly he is demanding and from whom. Neil and I stay frozen in surprise. We would never expect something like that from Steve. The man looks at him with exhausted, shy eyes.

Man: We have to do it. My son, we have to do it.

Steve lets go of him. The man walks away without another word.

Neil: And then you say your neighbour is mad. The whole thing runs like an asylum. Let's go with them. Let's hear the speech. We will see your time mover later.

We join the crowd. We follow them to the main square. A woman of no more than thirty is making a speech. She has a thin, pale face, wears a khaki jacket and a lousy pair of jeans; her voice, though, is stable and strong.

Woman in Khaki: Dear compatriots, we do not live in the dark ages of despair and terror; do not think this way; we live the cynicism, accompanied by a strange piety. Cynicism is our capital, but piety is the maintenance of our spiritualised surveyance state. Capital was used to be dead labour that, vampire like, breathed sacrificing living men, and existed the more, the more living men it sacrificed.

The crowd moves with uneases. The woman continues.

Woman in Khaki: There is no longer any need for such belief, everything is preformed, arranged in advance. Capital is the living labour nowadays, the cannibal, fuelled by dead corpses. Causality is reversed, evolution shattered. We are the stock of exploitation. To be more precise, the useless stock of exploitation. We are fast transformed to a stateless monetary mass. We are the overflow of our voluntary servitude. We are abandoned to erratic work or to unemployment food vouchers. We are the living dead, feeding a broken machine, a discarded gear.

The crowd starts to shout: stop feeding us the dead! *The woman in the khaki's voice repeats:* Stop feeding us the dead!

Neil: Let's go away. We have seen enough.

Me: It's an open secret then.

Neil: Exactly. It seems everybody knows. We eat the dead. We have fallen into the stock waste department. That's it. The floats stopped. A closed vessel of no use.

Me: And our piety? Eating the dead. Indeed smart. No more waste in the waste box. We are fully self-sustainable.

Neil: Very nutritious indeed.

Neil's attitude breaks my sanity. I feel like I want to run at him and smash his head with mine. Steve intervenes.

Steve: Let's see what our time mover knows.

We walk fast from the main square to the avenue, turn left to a narrow filthy road and then cross the small park. 'The Heliconian spring on frail foundations lay, in earthly mould,' I say to myself.

She is sitting on her small sofa, her hands bound in her lap, her hair combed tight in a low pony tail.

Wise woman: We had long heard tell of whole worlds vanishing, of empires sunk without a trace, gone down with all their men and all their machines into the unexplorable depths of the centuries, with all their gods and laws.

She takes a small breath and continues.

Wise woman: We were aware that the visible earth is made of ashes and the ashes signify something. And there we are, we now know civilisation has the same fragility as life.

Steve: Wise woman forgive us; your words have shaken my heart. Give your commands as you gave your words and we shall follow our destiny.

Me: Please. I know your words; I read them long ago; a lecture of a man, I do not remember of which century.

Wise woman: Oh, dear. Of course, they are not my words, as nothing else in the text. I am not real for your time to be. I am only a Generatrice, a mechanic reproduction of printed knowledge. Although that makes me no less important. Follow my instructions or you die. Horrors would never have been possible without so many virtues. Science needed to kill so many. Science needed to annihilate so many cities. The facts are clear and pitiless.

Steve: It is the consciousness of terror?

Wise woman: Yes, my son, that's it. A trans-universality of one's reason.

Steve: We will not legitimise the arbitrary despotism. We will fight the enemy.

Steve holds her hand in his own.

Wise woman: First you have to understand the enemy. It might have a nerve system; it might have a centre of concentration and power. Consider a map of the world. Then consider a map of time. In this time-sphere are all inhabitable lands. The whole is divided into regions and in each region, in each timeslot, there is a certain density of evil and a certain quality of good. In each of these regions there are also substratum of more or less influence. Now we shall classify history of the next moment given the inequality. We have foreseen a gradual change in the opposite direction. This is an enterprise requiring gifts that, when found together, are usually the most incompatible. It requires Argonauts of the mind. Tough pilots, who refused to be either lost in their thoughts or distracted by their impressions. Neither the frailty of the premises that supported them, nor the infinite number and subtlety of the inferences they explored, could dismay them. A space itself, became from century to century, as though gaining possession of itself, confidence of reason and original intuition, by its own reaction, bound to change by degrees into an imbalance in the opposite direction. Seeking freedom against the conspiracy of things. We may create this freedom. Yes, it is possible.

She looks like a strange puppet, in her absurdity of speech. Steve and Neil are charmed. I doubt her; for reason's sake; I remember this passage, only somehow differently. It sounds as if it has been mixed up, abridged. May I say? Totally messed. Yes, I remember very well now; it is from the old times before the distortion. What is she trying to say?

Wise woman: Matralia is the day. Mithras needs his offerings. But I give you the Ancillae; move fast when the dawn rises; you have only three days. Get the key, which is a manifestation of the sixth king. Servus non habet personam. The temple of Feronia is your new duel.

Troy: Rome

Neil: My gosh, look at that girl; they have beaten her near to death.

A man passed near us.

Man: She is just a prostitute. Nothing of importance. She will get laid for a glass of cheap wine and with her ugly looks, even that is hard to find. Such a filthy creature. Do you see her? Full of scars and dry skin. Sickening really.

The girl is bleeding quietly. Steve walks towards her; he tries to hold her hand. As she opens her fingers, a small cross slips to the ground. The girl makes an effort to get her cross back. Steve gives it to her.

Steve: Do not be afraid my dear. We are going to keep you safe.

She seems not to understand. She doesn't move at all. We see no fear on her face, no despair, only a faint glimpse of nothingness, holding her eyes to the sky. Steve takes her in his arms.

Steve: Bloody hell.

We see the temple. A priest is taking care of the candles in the outer doors. Steve walks near him.

Steve: Move us to the sacred chamber.

The priest obeys.

Priest: The twelve tablets.

The priest sarches the papyrus.

Priest: Here we are. Unfortunately, according to the fifth tablet, crucifixion awaits her.

Me: No. Give her the cap of Pileus. We will take her with us.

Priest: If you wish so.

The priest responds positively.

Priest: Does she have an ear piercing?

Me: I see nothing.

Priest: Good, that makes it easier.

He is relieved.

Priest: Ear piercing would have enslaved her forever, till death. First, we must wash her. Then dress her properly before she can have her Pileus.

We agree. We move to a nearby small building. White stone and bulky walls. A woman helps Steve and Neil to undress the girl and pour water over her bronzed body. She seems in pain, but she doesn't complain at all; she keeps her eyes closed.

Woman: Look, no bad damage. Except. Oh my gosh...

Then we see.

Woman: They burned her in her...

The woman doesn't say the word. She looks terrified as she walks out. We stay there, looking at each other.

Neil: What a cruel thing to do.

The woman returns. She covers the girl with a brown cream.

Woman: We better leave her to rest.

We leave her in a small bed near the bath.

Me: That's Rome.

Steve: Have you seen Troy?

Me: What?

Steve: The woman is wearing a cross around her neck; I saw it as she was bending over the girl's body.

Me: They start building the net.

Steve: We need them. We need their help. We must get his key.

Neil: We know; he is a stone king.

Me: Is it the action or the soul?

Steve: It depends.

Me: The hermeneutics of desire?

Steve: Desire? What does desire have to do with it? The woman has value only due to her virginity, to her purity. Without hymen she has been left to her chute. Prostitution is her useful fall.

Me: But it is always a possibility of redemption, isn't it?

Steve: I do not think so. In her case no. There is no such thing for her in this life, only perhaps in her next; her afterlife.

Neil: We all know; redemption for a woman is only a husband. And who will marry this poor creature?

Me: I will marry her.

Neil: For god's sake. We are here for a reason and you want to get married?

Me: Yes.

Neil: We have more important issues than carrying her around.

Me: I do not care. I will marry her. Now. After her Pileus ceremony.

Neil: Ok. Marry her; do whatever you want to do. Useless as always.

Me: Please. She deserves an opportunity to have some dignity.

Neil: I just said; do whatever you like, but we must find what we came to seek.

Steve: At the moment let her be tranquil and rest. She needs a good sleep and a proper dinner.

Me: What is missing? Something is missing.

The woman with the cross around her neck comes near.

Woman: There is also the way of Mary.

The woman speaks in a tranquil voice.

Woman: Freed from passion, fear and anger, absorbed in me, taking refuge in me, and purified by the fires of Knowledge, many have become one with my Being.

Steve: Oh, I know. The Omnipresent, the Incomprehensible, the Eternal.

Neil: Devoted then. The Saviour has a name?

Woman: The Divine Incarnation.

Me: Please. Lead us. We need to find our way out.

Woman: Help me and I will help you.

Me: What do you need?

Woman: All our goodness is a loan. God is the owner. God works, and his work is God.

Me: You just said that you need help.

Woman: Yes, I do. We do. We lay hidden in self-imprisonment. We worship God, hidden underneath the city, like scared rats, like human ghosts. He is a ruthless king. He kills us on fires, crosses and terrible tortures.

Me: One day you will do the same.

She opens her eyes wide.

Woman: No. Never. Please, do not say such horrific words.

Steve: Leave her alone.

Steve pushes me back.

Steve: We are here for a reason and this is not to debate the future. Remember there is a certain amount of good. Let's gain it. Let's be open enough to accept it.

Neil: The lamb case.

Steve: The slaughter case.

Me: The offer to God, or shall we call it the limit case?

The woman smiles. She takes my hand and kisses it.

Woman: Yes. The offer case; the perfect patience.

Steve: There is no such thing. We are only humans. Nothing more. We can never reach something beyond our reach.

Me: Yes, but at least we must be able to permit His grace on us.

The woman approaches me.

Woman: Up then noble soul! Put on thy jumping shoes which are intellect and love.

Neil: Ok. You got me. Let's try, even though we may lose.

56

We stay there three days and three nights; then our little bird had her ceremony and I took her as my wife. Poor little thing, she couldn't believe it. All evening she holds me tight to her body shaking softly like a shimmering star in a dark sky. Then the five of us move to the underworld. My wife is shining at this depth, beautiful like a secret flower, like earth's rose. Flourishing, day by day, to immense beauty. Her skin turns white and her cheeks light pink; her wound is almost cured now. She follows me like a happy little puppy, smiling and looking at me with tender eyes.

Neil: Look what some gentleness does to a woman. Almost unbelievable.

Me: Not to me. I knew it from the first moment I saw her. She will be fine. She is gaining self-esteem.

Neil: Of course, of course. The redemption worked. A small miracle.

Steve: For her it is not small; it's a new life. A bright new life. Do you know what drove her in the first place? She is such a pretty creature, what happened to her?

Me: No questions. I want her at ease. No interrogations. Only simple, pure happiness.

Steve: The others don't look so happy. They are tired of living in the darkness. Whole families, with small children who do not know the sun's light. Dear friends, it is time to do something.

Steve contradicts my tranquillity.

Neil: Yes. Time to get this city open to light. The army is falling. One by one the soldiers are moving to the cross. They prepare a new king. They just need a push.

Neil seems well informed.

Me: We need our key. As always, the problem of action is imposed. How to accede the environment without experiencing the inner terrors of a metamorphosis. Grandeur or servitude?

I look at both of my friends to see the impression of my words on them.

Neil: The first is appealing but fucking disastrous. Servitude will do us for a while. Then we move to freedom.

Neil is on his toes, ready to blow the wind.

Steve: Remember we have to understand the enemy. Let him lead. Let him do as he wishes. Then we manifest. Then we fool him in his own arrogance.

Me: We are the players as well as the cards and the stakes.

She comes near us, my wife, my Mary.

Mary: There is a dilemma and a choice. I love him because he never posed a dilemma, but he has made a choice. He calls me wife, but I never lie with him, although we sleep together every night. Our aim now is to survive. There is a personal issue, as there is a collective issue. We need both. There is a fundamental deformation of the

Great Truth. Union is not a past or a future. Union is a growth. Union is reflection upon itself. Union is a volume of being. Union communicates itself. We form the reflective centre. We must approach the fact.

She turns to me.

Mary: Troy, do not be afraid; I am your first aid. She moved the helpers. She will not let you alone. I will see you again when time leads us to the new zone, the new Spiral. The king will die tomorrow by Neil's knife. The blood will not stain his soul; he is a king without blood, his veins are made from freezing ice, from an era made by ice. He will kill a puppet, not a man. Like steam he will vanish in the air and then Steve can get the key of time. It is the power of the one that kills the will of the many. We don't follow; we participate. All of us. We don't lead; we create our lives. Step by step we create our lives. The realm of brotherhood is coming.

Troy: The Stone Man

We walk to his chambers. Mary, my sweet maiden, knows all about him. She knows his life, although she never posed him a question. He asked her to join him in his summer chambers. But first, he said, she had to pass his test of cruelty. She was surprised. What did that mean? Then she saw. The Christians were thrown as a mass of fleshy pain; they lay one on the top of the other, packed in small cells of misery; no water, no food, no dignity. Nothing but human terror made by lack and fear.

'Now,' *he said to her,* 'lead them to their destiny. You see they have the same inferior roots as yours. Slave's roots, but you are the lucky one. I made an exception and I gave you the caresses of my love. You see, my dear, I loved you once, many years ago, my sweet little bird, when you were my little girl and I was your prince of love. Now times have changed. You are a nothing coming from nothingness, a no destiny creature. The slave race, the lazy race of no worth. Prove to me that you deserve my hands on your body; prove to me that you deserve my bed. Go sweetheart and get them, all of them and lead them to the burning crosses of my death ceremony.'

She was terrified, but faithful to him; she took the chain and led the grieving mass to their fatal end. But when she reached the doors, when he was ready to accept her in his nuptial bed, she stepped in the opposite direction. The mob became uneasy; she was upset, her tears flowing, streams of dead passion and inner sorrow. She unleashed them. Everyone moved as fast as possible. People still not believing that the fresh air of freedom was here for them. Mothers with small children in their arms, grandfathers screaming amen to the skies. A young girl gave her a small cross with a small blue stone in the middle before she ran away. She stood there alone. He didn't stop her.

He said, 'all-right. Very well. That was my nuptial present. Now it is your turn.'

She was sealed with the burn. Then his men threw her into the prostitute's market where we found her. I hold her hand. She is smiling beautifully, like an angel. Her burn healed fast. She has been lucky; his commendatory was a young, smooth eyed man, he has tried not to harm her. He has done his job to the minimum. He was sorry to see her in such a pitiless condition.

We find him sitting on his throne; no one near him. 'I was expecting you,' *he says to Mary*, 'you and your husband and his shadowy friends. You intend to kill me, although I don't know how. As you know sweetheart, I am a man without blood, impossible to be killed by humans. As you know dear, I came out of a stone, made by stone. You may remember once we were together in love, in a forest made by forged trees and leaves of my heart's uneasiness. Once I set you free; a second time recently, I forgave your disobedience. And yet, instead of gratitude, you come back to kill me. How many lies have you told your friends? Do you describe facts and realities or your distorted visions? Did I ever kill any one of your sweet little friends underneath the earth? Of course, I knew where you stayed but I let you go free; I kicked you free, you little monster, to live as you wish. I took pity on you. Was I responsible for your burns? Was it my work? Are you sure about that? You are such a fool. Who are they? Creatures of your immense fantasy? Friends? You never had friends. Once you called yourself Hierophile, now Mary. What next? Let me guess; Hystaspes? A *sympeplegmenon* of essence. You are essence to me, but I am ice cold to you. An empty god. A god made from stone.'

'Yes,' *Mary says firmly*, 'that's exactly what you are'.

'Ask her to forgive you,' *Neil demands*.

'I do ask her to forgive me*,' the Stone Man replies.*

'Not with words, with actions,' *I command*.

He walks close to Mary, almost face to face, and he says: 'Love is her name, and light is her lane. Time is ripe. I am the one to go. She is the one to be. Let her be.'

Every dream has a shattered reality and every reality a shattered dream. He vanished in small steams, pulverised like fireflies in the trembling of the night's winds.

'Here is the key,' *Neil says happily*.

'Breathe the Eagle's flames. Heliodromus rises.'

As we take a deep breath my mind opens broken seals of isolation. Broken seals of a new will.

'Continue,' *the Stone Man's voice says to Mary, looping back as a stream of rapid flame coming out of nowhere,* 'Continue. Narrate. Narrate us all. Mercy mixed with no mercy; love with hate; good with evil. Breathe and clean all your deposits until the day of the freed will come. Get our possibillities now and move your squares. Your time's labyrinth, your living maze. Move carefully but not too slow. The thread is made by the same material as the maze. It is a *homoion*. The fountain awaits us. Move to the clear waters. We must re-wind the clock.'

Troy: The zero-player game (Alive or Dead?)

Arrested movement.
Me: Is it the Spiral's growth or the highway?
Steve: I prefer ants, Troy.
Neil: Better the left and right edges of the field to be stitched together, and the top and bottom edges also, feeding a toroidal array.
Me: That's ridiculous Neil. Better keep it simple.
Neil: We are going to get lost. It's getting fucking chaotic.
Me: Thus, why I said keep it simple.
Steve: It's your glider gun, Neil. It causes a series of new mutations.
Neil: They are not mutations. Timeslots. You said already we play reality. Remember, dead or alive.
Me: We must save memory. Do you hear me? Save some memory for the end. We will not be able to escape.
Steve: We will be trapped.
Neil: But we have to explore the pattern to the fullest.
Steve: It is impossible; it keeps growing out of scope.
Me: It's never out of scope.
Steve: But the vast majority are either too chaotic or too desolate to be of any interest.
Me: I know, that's why we get the spaceship.
Steve: Move around the ants. The immigration games. Eliminate the opponent's cells.
Me: We have fallen into a flip.
Neil: Turn left Troy. I said left.
Steve: For god's sake it is an attractor; we will never be able to get out.
Neil: Only 154 steps. My manual says so. It's not infinite; only 7 paths of ampler sound, repeating 22 times each.
Me: You said that already.

Neil: Move back to the highway.

Steve: I can't.

Neil: Make an extension to a qualified plane. That's the secret. Time is only another dimension of space. Then we are out.

Steve: Which Spiral?

Neil: I do not know. Whatever. We don't have a choice right now. We think about it later. *Circular causality and the specific freezing point.*

Me: The Egg. That's it. We fill the Egg. Neil is encapsulated. He is closing himself in the Egg.

Steve: It is the illusion state. Is there any way to break it?

Me: No. I think he will get out in a while, but without the memory of its plane.

Steve: Nothing serious then.

Me: No, not really. Only a crack in the space.

Steve: The Egg, then, is not our reality?

Me: I do not think so.

Steve: Is it the mass of the forces?

Me: The concentration point. But not the final reality.

Steve: We search for the exit.

Me: That's the whole of our purpose. We must find the exit to creation. We simulate the whole system, modelling time into calculus. We need an infinite life span.

Steve: Is it possible then? The universals are possible?

Me: Ignore the limitations of finite memory. Use an arbitrary multiplexer.

Steve: I can't; it keeps falling apart. The incompleteness of the decision problem.

Me: Do not decide then. Make the branches unconditional.

Steve: I have a fear that it's a loop. Recursive functioning.

Me: Oh please. An oracle with random data is non-computable.

Steve: How many oracles do we need to provide unconditional calculations?

Me: Wrong question. You could go on and never get to an end.

Steve: High life only asserts replicators.

Me: Try a lucky chance.

Steve: I said we search for the thread of luck, not of her chance.

Me: Then we are back to the same question. Is it all about memory? Are we circuiting time or memory?

Steve: Can a dead cell be born? Attention! We just fell into abstractors.

Me: Take the oscillators. Make a pulsar; then you have time. Make time blink. Create your pattern; then you have memory.

Steve: How many cells? How many generations?
Me: I don't care. It is the seed that I am interested in.
Neil: Fuck both of you. I don't care for your seed. I need an exit point. And I need it now.
Me: Shut it down then.
Neil: The old reboot thing.
Steve: At least we got him back.
Neil: Whom?
Steve: You.
Neil: Why? Did I go someplace and don't know it? We are stuck in this console for days.
Me: Please Steve, drop the conversation; he has no clue; memory gap. It's normal.
Neil: Are you mad or what?
Steve: I worried for a moment, but yes, we are all together again.
Neil: Ok then, the burning flames of the Eagle and the Oracle is on the moon. Fasten your seatbelts brothers, we are only a few moments away.

Hierophile: The moon

Fate loves to invent patterns and designs. The woman is the Oracle itself, and it is Time that speaks through her. The woman who is in love always surpasses the man she loves, because life is greater than fate. Her devotion wants to be immense: this is her bliss. But the nameless sorrow of her love has always been this: that what is asked of her is that her devotion must be kept within limits.

The difficulty dwells in its complexity. But life itself is hard because of its simplicity. Natural selection is sufficient to explain the apparent functionality and non-random complexity of the biological world and can be said to play the role of watchmaker in nature, albeit as an automatic, unintelligent, blind watchmaker. I keep a note: The mega mechanical tree; no matter if roots are freed or not, if branches are burnt or not; what matters is the inherent rule. I think we call it Law.

Womb was a misconception, at least in the upper level. The flat opus. Chora. Not a mirror, neither a substance. Womb, seed, and the rest apply only to space and time. I mean what the hell; in the beginning, loneliness had no name. I am not sure. I was once. In the Orphic texts Phanes is the name of the egg that Nyx gave birth. Nyx, the bird with black wings fertilised by the primordial wind Ether; she gave birth to a silver egg. From the egg Eros came into life. His other names are Phanes, Protogonos, Metis, Herikepaios. He had four eyes, four horns, and golden wings.

Hoarse like a Bull and a Lion, a woman in front and a man behind. Protogonos carries the divine seed.

The unexplainable connection, a geology of psychic fossils, appearing as a memory's stratification; I am only reading what I can already recognise, like I am following a line, a pivot, an axis, and every time, I add one more little pebble to the image. A curtain that separates me from life in her shadow. Not only an uncured disease, nothing to fight, nothing to accept, only the sharp sound of isolation.

Hierophile: Hold me in your arms a moment and I will dance, a bee fluttering my wings. *Potnia* Muse, my thought rises at yours; shall I ask for wind or rain in the raven's mires of shade? In the moon I had only one wish: to grow wings. As the wings grew, my body was pinned in the lunar desert. The volcano is my shelter. A shelter made by ashes. There I am in my fetters, bound for an eternity.

He approaches; the face of an Eagle, the body of a Man.

Horus: I didn't come to save you. Spectres we of the dead hours be. We bear Time to his tomb in eternity. Solid as crystal, yet through all its mass, sphere within sphere and every space between.

Horus: Who ministered to Thebes, Heaven's poisoned wine. Unnatural love, and more unnatural hate. These shall perform your task: Strange combinations out of common things.

Hierophile: You hear the thunder of my new wings? The space within my plumes darker than night? Mingled with love and then dissolved in sound? My world spinning in pain.

Horus: The boundless element; where the wild bee never flew. Through the noontide darkness, deep by the odour-breathing sleep of faint night-flowers and the waves at the fountain-lighted caves. Nor form, nor outline is gazed on another's eye.

He came forth upon my lips.

Horus: I wish no living thing to suffer pain. Equal, unclassed, tribeless, and nationless. To love and bear; to hope, till Hope creates.

The beauty of his eyes broke silence and space. Liquidating all fetters to a new desire.

Horus: I am not made from desire. I am your guide, follow my flight. Harmony will gather us all in the deep universe caverns.

Hierophile: Verses of love

A vine. A laurel. A new birth. Mithras is dead. I find the exit. He has vanished, like a phantom, out of my thought. I am again back. Under the sun. Not a pitiless sun.

Not at all. A tender watcher. Rome has vanished with him. The Empire is falling into forgetfulness. Joy is my new day. Let him kiss me with the kisses of his mouth. We fall into a beautiful land. We pass the seven planets.

He says, 'No tolls. You must pay no tolls. The shipmen decided so. We will move towards the landscapes of thought. Get clothed in me; wrapped up in my skin. Do not be afraid. Time forgot to run those lands. Time is not your destiny. Break all forms, time, space, causality. Break the terrors of the three-horned monster. Until I reach the watch house of Fire. Until I reach the watch house of The Seven. Until I reach the water brooks. Take my palm and follow my flight. Set me on the arms of immortal life. I am offering my heart as I invoke the end of the universe. This is your grace. Hold my hand tight. Open your wings now. Open them. Fly near me. Fly on me. Make me your infinite joy. Make me your glory.'

My wings are lifted up high. Because you have removed my fetters from me. My lover, you raised me out of the frozen darkness. I am lifted up and I approach you. Like a dream he whispers:

Living shapes upon my bosom move, winged

Dark with the rain new buds are dreaming of:

This is love, all love!

My measure is full, I say to my lover. They closed the gates before me. But I raised my eyes on high. I looked out and beheld the House of Life; Clothed with radiance.

Troy: The Trident

Steve: She is moving fast Troy.
Me: Yes, I know; is she in a hurry or just in good luck?
Steve: I don't know.
Neil: But we are not so lucky. They may ask for tolls.
Me: You see them?
Neil: The Watchers?
Me: Yes.
Neil: You little monks of fear, I have nothing to pay them. We paid our debts, for generations. So many generations paid for us. We pass for free.
Me: How is that possible?
Neil: You will see Troy, you will see. Is Mary with you, or Drusiana, or whatever you call her?

Me: Luckily enough, Anisidor is with us. Mary will get on board later. We need to reactivate her.

Neil: Of course, Anisidor. He is the body of the new cosmos. Isn't he?

Steve: We cannot do anything without him.

Neil: I know. This is his wreckage of a ship? I thought it had capsized.

Me: Oh please. You are ready to make a fuss of everything and a joke of everything. It's a good old ship, keep your comments to yourself.

Steve: Boys please, enough for today.

Neil: Do I have to pass all this mingled with nothingness darkness and not laugh about my sky trip?

Steve: At least we have a ship Neil.

Me: We have no other option.

Neil: Do we really have to call this bloody machinery a ship?

Anisidor: Welcome to my ship Neil. Welcome boys; be my guests.

Neil: The captain has joined us.

Neil's manners are so rude sometimes; his raw sense of humour.

Me: Mind your manners Neil.

Neil: For god's sake, it's a relief. I meant nothing bad.

Anisidor: The same danger basted on us as in the forest of the Unknown. We were lucky that the Eagle intervened; usually he doesn't do so. She would have been lost if he had kept his solitary expression. His distant ways will not have saved her from the double helix. The fetters were double bounded, worked with wise patience and extreme cunningness.

Neil: You speak about Drusiana? She was simply lucky.

Anisidor: Drusiana will get on board later. I speak of Hierophile, the Oracle.

Me: Are you sure? Was she lucky?

Steve: This wasn't part of the plan for salvation?

Neil: I don't think so.

Steve: I think so.

Anisidor: We are all part of the plan.

Neil: What about you Anisidor? Are you also part of the plan? You do not exist in any place and yet you are the captain on our journey. Then is Mary or Drusiana or whatever you call her; is she really Troy's wife, or your mistress?

Anisidor: Please Neil, do not offend me and do not speak nonsense.

Neil retreats abruptly from the conversation and throws himself on the deck, keeping his eyes closed.

Anisidor: The secret is to stop denying, to accept, and then float to the transparent waters of existence.

Me: But it is an empty longing. The beginning; the start, has nothing human, is an endless incoherence.

Anisidor: Troy, my boy, perhaps your labyrinthine existence is the incoherence.

Me: Human being is an object to be cancelled.

Steve: Action as a limit?

Me: A boundary marker.

Steve: But it's all of us together that make the song.

Anisidor: Let me tell you my story.

Anisidor interrupts the conversation, and at the same time takes the rudder in his hands.

Neil: You are most welcome.

Neil surprises us with his gentle manner and opens his eyes.

Anisidor: While you were searching for a way out of Mithras' spell, I was searching for a way back to the beginning. I was sailing in the vast northern seas; those are deadly seas, known among sailors as the ghosts' seas of miraculous hazards; that was when I first came across mermaids.

Anisidor narrates in a trembling voice, looking ahead at the horizons flickering lights. At the same time, he is manoeuvring our ship among gigantic electrified waves. He smoothly avoids their negatively charged, foaming tails; embroidered as they are with crystalloid grids of solid structure. Each time a cloud of protons is fused among them, we get carried away by the strong magnetic winds. Anisidor channels the ship quickly back onto the right frame without much of an effort. Neil bursts out laughing.

Neil: I love your sailor stories Anisidor, please go on.

Anisidor: Mermaids are not to be laughed at Neil. Nor can they be conceived as simply mythical creatures. They are half primitive figures of dead eras and half living humans of no such conscience.

His voice is charged with tension, a worn-out chord, vibrating the frictions breaking into the thick air covering our ship.

Neil: Oh please, I am disinclined to believe in children's fairy tales.

Neil scoffs at Anisidor's speech furiously.

Me: Stop it Neil. Let Anisidor speak.

I feel irritated. From time to time Neil upsets me with his stubborn attitude of knowing about almost everything. Neil lies back on the deck again, pretending that he has fallen asleep.

Steve: Come on, Troy, be quiet; you are more of a mess than Neil sometimes.

Steve throws himself next to Neil, punching his ribs slightly, obliging him to reopen his eyes. Neil pushes him cheerfully, knocking on his chest.

Neil: Come on, come on, let's see who's the strongest.

Steve: You are.

Steve retreats.

Steve: I'd rather listen to the story.

Neil: Let me sleep then, coward.

Neil lies back for a second time in his pretentious indifference, eyes closed.

Anisidor: Mermaids.

Anisidor continues, then pauses for a moment as though making sure that we will keep our mouths shut and finally takes his phrase from the beginning.

Anisidor: Mermaids signify the self-violation, the resistant suffering material of cosmos. They float among fallen ice rocks and skull bones. They do not speak. They talk only in music. They wonder. Sometimes they look deeply into the sailors' galvanized eyes and a promise of happiness falls from their eyelids. Purple, beautiful eyes open, their colours like souls dancing over astral nights. The most authentic, intense experience surprises their smiles. Strong in their excess of emotion, they come close to the lonely vessels and open their arms of beauty, ready to master the floating ships to their nocturne will. Innocence is the most imprudent act of their beautiful hearts. Instinct of freedom. Their whole being is an incarnation of this very instinct. Purity of freedom. Divided-self, made by deep, dark waters and human flesh partaking eternity. What an absolute immanent beauty. Here we were.

Anisidor takes a breath and then speaks again.

Anisidor: Floating among them, watching their fictitious songs. Oh, because their songs are not real. Mystical flowers are reaching our ears from inside. There is no sound, nothing to press upon atmosphere, no wave, only that our minds were synchronised with their tone of density; music spreads its leaves from inner fields, like petals opening in the morning dew. Aware as we are that those creatures of incarnated beauty have one and only attitude: captivity. Aware that inside them lies the original conflict of making meaning through their only real state of freedom, which is love. You see, their fundamental self seeks to absorb the other, the foreigner, the alien. Only we, the others, can serve as their means of freedom, by our own assimilation, our voluntary fall into their magnetic charm, into their fascinating existence. In the joy of their love, in the bliss of their deadly hug around our bodies, we were the means to justify their existence. The whole enterprise of seduction is just a frantic look. Look at us. Look at us and surrender. Bound with us to the vastest regions of the worlds. We are a world all for you.

We are listening in silence; Anisidor continues, keeping his talk fast paced.

Anisidor: My ship was old and the crew tired from the seas elongated distances; their song gave such a wonderful promise. Those shimmering eyes were opening lands of graceful serenity. We were ready to fall into their hands, ready to fall into their hunting jaws. A painful unity is their purpose, the final communion. We risked ourselves by longing for them. Drusiana was among my crew those days. I remember her, clothed as she was in a long, white dress, walking astern, touching the salty wet wood of the old hull with her thin, gentle hands, leaning the sweetness of her emerald gaze into the deep waters. She spoke to the mermaids with no trace of trembling, no trace of fear in her voice and she said:

In love I came across horror,
In horror I discovered sorrow,
In sorrow I found that reality is my shade
In my shade I saw the world spinning around my vertex
In my vertex I felt my spine aching like a growing tree of nothingness
In nothingness I met him
But he betrayed me.
In nothingness I felt at home
And my home was made of green ivy
A strange chain of paths whirling in each other and I found myself in it.
I was obliged to walk although I knew nothing
I was obliged to obey although I knew not whom
I was obliged to discipline although I knew not the aim
And then I saw a small light, a whispering light, and I said that must be called psyche, a small butterfly, a tender word of delight.
But I doubted, and I melted her between my fingers.
I found myself in a darkness that was repeated in infinite spaces.
I was doubled and then split again and then I was repeatedly separated like uncountable distance.
I was distance for myself.
And I found that in distance a space was created, a space all for me.
There I stood.
A reflection, an inclination, a drift.
But inside me was moving the flavour of darkness

But inside me was a glimpse of memory
And I said *may my word be reality*
May my reality be word.
And all my space was reversed and then collapsed like a falling arm
An arm ready to reach creation.
When she had said all she had to say, Drusiana stayed steel and silent. The mermaids are now in tears. An ocean groans on our sky. An icy earth grips our hearts.

'Is it life or death we are searching for?' I ask her.

'In death there are no spectators. In death, there is no fire. In death, divinity is a lonely dream of fear. But here in this small, carnal stain of emotion that is called human; here is also a portion of reason that is called nous and we are his vessel of self-definition, of self-awareness. Move then and break the isolation. Alienation is only the first of the paths to be walked; the next is the sphere of recovered mysteries, the handling of our own salvation. Find the torch, the key and the rod. Find the square, the spindle and the mnemonic. Make craft an art, and oblivion a memory. And from memory, run towards the deathless land. Creation is our womb, and time is our unbound fetters.'

Anisidor takes a breath and looks at his compass.

Anisidor: We are on our way.

We stay silent for a while, looking ahead at the flickering lights on the horizon. Anisidor's story is pressing upon our happy endeavour. Waves of stellar energy are moving our ship fast towards the Fire Gates. Neil seems worried.

Neil: We are ready to crash our vessel on a sky trip towards a deadly Watchman. What help is that at all?

Anisidor: Look boy, we have the mermaids' Trident in our hands. The fountain of the ocean.

Neil looks at the Trident with ecstatic eyes.

Neil: Yes, that makes sense and bloody hell, that is fucking helpful. Let me kick this bad ass.

Steve: Relax Neil; we are not here to play the fighting boys.

Me: Let's see what the Fire Watcher is all about. Reactivate Drusiana, Steve.

Steve walks fast into his console. Neil gets the Trident.

Troy: The Fire Watcher and the Promise

Drusiana: Hold your breath.

Drusiana screams. Neil holds the glorious trident tight in his hand. Anisidor turns the ship straight to the Fire Gates. The Watcher looks at us. He has a child's face, crystal whiteness in his eyes. He is young and seems somewhat absent minded. As we come closer, he half opens the gates and asks for tolls.

Fire Watcher: Silver souls. I want a thousand silver souls for my evening supper. You will never pass if you don't pay me.

His eyes change colour from crystalline to dark green. His cheeks are now reddish. His lips move as though ready to cast a curse. Neil runs fast and pierces his forehead with the first tooth of the mermaid's trident. The Watcher speaks with a sweet girly voice.

Fire Watcher to Neil: You small idiot. It is not possible to harm me; you can only delay me for a while; your trident is not the way to get me; it is only a move before your final destruction, but here it is my rule: if you don't feed me with living souls you can always feed me with your living bodies.

Fire Watcher to Anisidor: I cannot compete with a non-existent body like yours, Anisidor, neither with your shadow fiancée; you can pass if you wish so; it will change nothing, but here you have three living sailors and they're pretty delicious for my taste.

Drusiana: He is suffocating from desire. His aim is ensnarement of your bodies. He needs flesh to incarnate himself as flesh.

Fire Watcher: Oh, dear Mary.

The Fire Watcher says, approaching Drusiana, the distance of a breath, though calling her Mary.

Fire Watcher to Drusiana: Is it you who is speaking of traps while you are made as an entrapment for Anisidor? You dare to speak and give advice to three morons that have no clue how to divide a game correctly and move to the next level or platform or whatever they call it? Is it you, their little machine of prediction's absurdity, a hologram from their glitter gun, that dare to speak about my intention to alter state? They do not even know how to move to the first new zone of squares; they stayed back at the end of their little encapsulated zone and they dreamed to get to the outer space? Such an enormous mission: create time, create destiny, create their own fate. You know what they create? A loop. They loop around their tail. A big horrible laughter. That's all they created till now. Squares are only a part of the secret.

Fire Watcher to Me: Troy. You cannot solve the riddle. Mehen is a complicated game. I am here, totally bored, living in the Kingdom of Lonesome. And here you are, an adventurer, a space sailor! I give you an opportunity - take it or feel fire to your bones. Join me in the battle.

Steve: Be careful; something stinks badly here.

Neil: Hidden movements. That was our mistake; we didn't take into account the hidden movements.

Me: What shall we do now?

Neil: Join him; we have no other option.

Neil seems certain. I have no other option than to join him in battle.

Fire Watcher: I am going to introduce myself, dear adversary. My nature is synthetic; I am a synthetic form of life. I have been formed through desire. I was shaped in the form of desire. Every time a soul falls in my dish, I get a new cover, but souls are such lousy things, small and frightened; they last only a few seconds and are not enough to fill my appetite; I need lots of them just for a moment of a passing satisfaction. But a full body is such a beautiful delicacy, a wonderful change. I am so bored eating the same food all the time, centuries now, cursed in those lower regions of darkness, in this lonely nowhere. Join me and feed me; what a wonderfully brilliant good luck.

Neil: He speaks too much; pity we don't have a gun to send him our greetings with a lovely bullet.

Steve: Let's start. The structure is simple; we must move through different formations and transcend space as reflections of energy.

Neil: What the hell. A pure contingency, we need the splitter. Get ready, Troy. We move to a new property, we change the procedures and the definition.

Me: Is he a virus?

Steve: No something more advanced, a guardian; that means he keeps the limits of the border safe; he does not allow life to trespass. He is the first shadow maker, the first to our way for the iron curtain. We will be at the defence line; move yourself in front; attack, do not transcend; attack him straight in his primary substance.

Me: Provided that I have the right weapon.

Steve: Of course, here it is. A stratified opening. Reflect him to the underworld; we recoil time, three square zones up. Here you will find a gap to push him into.

Me: It's the Trident.

Steve: Exactly. It has the shape of a trident. Push him six squares left and one up. That's it. That's it.

Neil: Great, he has fallen in the pit.

Me: Is it a garbage collector?

Neil: No. No waste here. Call it recycling.

Neil couldn't stop laughing. That was a great battle. A few squares, a trident and a beautiful gap. I love it.

Neil: What was all the nonsense about desire for?

Steve: Nothing really; they get a type of flesh through a mischievous procedure of stealing; they call it desire; it has to do with reproduction, but they have assimilated all wrong.

Me: Their sexual appetite blended with energy sources.

Neil: Hell, that's not clever at all.

Steve: It works with what they call soul; but full bodies are fields of escape, and they knew nothing about it.

Me: Lucky us.

Neil: Lucky you.

Anisidor: Shall we go on now?

Anisidor brings his strong body near us.

Drusiana: First, we must make a promise. We have to promise to submerge in one manifestation when the pleroma arrives. Remember where we have started from. Never forget the beginning. The Oracle has to re-join with the Herdsman.

Steve: He is really a Herdsman?

Drusiana: It is just another metaphor, a signal marker. He is near her, although he is always passing from new stratums. I speak for his final contact. There they will unite again in the prophecy. When the time for unity comes, we will be, all of us, their one and only manifestation. The goal will justify the act in her grace. In the origin we will have to face the end. But we must be ready for the unpredictable. There is always a possibility of error. We might have been mistaken. Necessity is a moving image of freedom. It is always possible to elapse or be revealed anew. The interpretation is not enough of an instrument. Reality is stronger.

Steve: And Horus?

Drusiana: Horus is not in our reach; we have to wait; it might be an aid or it will apply to indifference. We shall see. He is out of our scope; he has his own.

Steve: Shall we trust him?

Drusiana: I think so. But we cannot count on him. We know nothing of his nature. At the moment he is a great help; she moves fast, no tolls, what else to demand? It's already a rupture from pain and that is important.

Steve: But not enough. I am afraid of some state of degeneration.

Drusiana: Do not worry; she earns time. Until then we will be able to solve the riddle and move to the next literal space.

Neil: Wonderful. That is our purpose, the time given; we have to conclude the final eruption. Then is a new era and a new story.

A promise is made.

Troy: The House of the Seven or the Spiritual Realm

Me: The first appearance can be actual and at the same time potential, although it is always a revelation. The pillars are the joint point. Earth, Heaven and Underworld. We are in search of the original Universal Matrix. The first step is a tree construction. Remember, we cannot take anything back, although we must make certain that we are not reduced to breathing shadows. The whole domain leads to a bridge construction.

Make sure to exchange will with feeling and feeling with knowledge. It's the Beyond that we are searching for. We don't abandon Self, but we do not hold onto it either. It's an intermediate vision. Neither Essence nor Existence. Steve takes his manual and starts drawing a diagram of instructions.

Steve: I am going to rebuild the whole tree construction. Neil will have to use the tool of Protogonos as an action of Theogony. He has to use the square-meter as a tablet of assurance. All our moves are passing through this tablet. Life is the name of the first square. Death is the name of the second. But here we are; we come forth with a third name Truth, which validates the two previous ones. We have two pools to recharge our tablets, Lethe and Mnemosyne. We need both occasionally. Remember the pyres; we must eliminate each of them before we come across the House. We will meet the Oracle after the Brooks, near by the Lacuna. We are alone until then. Troy, here we have two possibilities to discharge. You get them. The first: The Ground of Reality. The second: The Sky of Illusion. Do not forget it is the war that nourishes war. Please, keep also in mind that the House is a winged disk; in the centre lies the Eye.

Drusiana: You need to create a Toxon. You will need Anisidor to cross the border and visualise the sphere. We will be enclosed once again for only a few moments; there is your chance. The Seven archons can appear in four different forms: Men, Lions, Oxen and Eagles. They all belong to the incorruptible race. As you move from one tree to the other, the patterns will form new consistencies. Mother was once part of them; she was called Eden in those days. The world will remain to her possession; we will only behold time for a while and pass through the net to be able to reach Omphalos. Do not mess up with Eden; you will be determined to lose. You can only cross through her; nothing more. The two-sided process will anoint merely a phantom of a body; Anisidor will have to be seized to install a new time assembly. But that will come later.

Neil: What about Mithras?

Drusiana: We must pay attention; he is a dangerous beast when he groans his descent. He has no consort. Thus, he does not belong to the Aeons. Mother devalued him. She has cast him into the places of conflict.

Me: And her insane son?

Drusiana: It is an unimpeded passage. We know nothing.

Me: Let's make a resume: We have two points of doubt and no knowledge, Horus and the Mother's son. At the moment, out of our immediate concern. We have a place of battle called the House of Seven. Two sources of energy and two for discharging. Three Squares. One used for validation. A tool box named Protogonos. A cross area named Eden or Mother's inhabitation, formed from chains of trees. A descended covering, Mithras. Helpers named Aeons but not yet under reach since they are in the outer sphere.

Drusiana: You forgot to mention Anisidor's Chariot and The Seven's different Faces. The Faces constitute classes of perceptions. Each perception - Face - will determine a weapon of fight. But you must make sure; here is no evil. You don't fight evil. The Seven do not represent evil; they are part of the Law. They are constructed as law, and are part of the map. You will only have to cross, that is, to pass through the Eye. The Seven are not obstacles; they are guardians. Remember there are no pit holes. They are guardians both of safety, and to the limit; both of freedom and imprisonment. They will form their patterns depending on your skills. If you know how to move, they will move accordingly. They do not deny self-consciousness. They deny blindness. They will let us move, only if we have the ability to cross, to break through.

Steve: All right. Everybody get ready. Neil will map Theogony by commanding through Protogonos' tool kit. It is a great platform of multiple realities and illusions, a Multispectrum-Theasis, a panoptic. Troy, fill the energy vouchers; I am ready to construct the tree realms. I will start from root One and move to the Second through Extinction. The Chariot is ready. Get it and prepare the Toxon to pass through the House's Eye. It is winged and that makes it kind of difficult, a moving target; your weapon has to run a curve and then stabilise in the Iris.

Neil: What are we going to do with the Faces? Seven to four makes twenty-eight distinct occasions.

Drusiana: Leave it to me. I will get them by subtraction.

Anisidor flies his sky ship into the dark wings of the horizontal flux, reaching the House, bold as a thundering rage. Iris has closed in an instant movement. The Seven is a substance deprived of meaning. That is new. We didn't take this into account when our plans were put into action.

Neil: We lose *Ektases*. We must rethink our interpretation. Regress into the past. Fast. Use Mnemosyne.

Me: I am, that's exactly what I'm doing.

Steve: Great. Forget linear determinism; forget vertical ascend; get the patterns of mystical recovery. The Seven are attacking us, combined into one. Be cautious. The state of unrevealed drives to a type of sharp contact. The foundation coincides with nothingness.

Neil: Ok then. Time to enable Theogony and bring Illusion into play.

Steve: Disavow the basement; renege the summit and fill the platform to be both autonomous and viable.

Seven: Not being birds, how do you propose we nest on an abyss?

Me: Who said that?

Seven: Me, the Ox and the Lion.

Me: Theogony works.

Steve: Of course, it always does.

Neil: Where are your two other Faces?

Seven: Men and Eagles are both in the game.

Me: I see no one.

Seven: Oh, you silly boy. You don't see your own definition. Look, the screen has two sides. On the other side are you, Men, and your Eagles of Fire. We are on the same platform, all of us. We all form the master of the House.

Steve moves a blocker. The Seven change their mode. The Mute State is not, though, less perilous.

Steve: Pay attention. They use us, against us. They are recapturing our movements, transforming them to their own substance.

Drusiana falls fast into the rupture and disqualifies The Seven's occasions.

Neil: Great. She is doing well.

Steve: Our fear is; what if they force us to fulfil their own command?

Me: The gory circle is alive; they know of no prohibition.

Steve: Overcoming gravity now.

Me: I did it.

Steve: Ok, keep up in the same layer.

Neil: Reduce the substance to his former shape.

Steve: We have to reopen the Iris and cross as a Toxon.

Me: Neil, only Neil can reform the eye.

Neil: Is it an assemblage? We must consider the connection points and the rubric.

Steve: Future strives against present.

Me: We are not forming a domino made of causes, motives and ends.

Steve: Forget it.

Neil: We are using Lethe to remove them and instead we fall into reality and we re-establish them.

Steve: The new transformation will get them into their core of existence.

Me: Keep them from multiplying. If they multiply, we run into Death's web.

Steve: The squares are forming emptiness. I never thought this could happen.

Me: Please, Steve, solve it fast; we need the Iris open; we cannot restrain them for much longer.

Steve: We a have series of death squares while life squares seem impenetrable.

Neil: I can't use our validation since Truth has nothing to confirm on death squares. I cannot apprehend the particular state. It comes like a series of zero's and nothing else. How do I validate it?

Steve: They are denying the future?

Neil: Yes. In some way they deny alteration and as a consequence future.

Me: Awaiting death then?

Neil: I am my own possibility.

Neil reopens Protogonos.

Neil: Let's hammer some original Freedom. Reverse all to one, Steve, and cause an overflow. Propel us on the ebb's stream Troy. Fast. Use your vouchers now.

The Toxon has been formed. Anisidor flies his sky ship on the top and we cross the Iris in full triumph; but we have lost Drusiana. Anisidor is filled with deep sorrow as we pass victoriously through the darkness and we are moving fast towards the Brooks.

Anisidor: We lost our Fidelity. We lost her. We have made known to ourselves a future, but we have lost our choice.

Neil: Everything happened in an instant; Nothingness consumed her in an unfolding of continuous Timelessness, breaking our unity. Our ship is intact, and we float towards destiny. Drusiana wasn't real; she never belonged to Reality.

Anisidor: Wrong. She might have been past but that doesn't make her unreal. She was part of the reality as disclosure, a grip on the past. You have to understand that choosing ourselves doesn't necessarily mean abandoning our past figures. We project both in the past and the future. It's not a one-way destination.

Steve: Maybe we will be able to find her. There must be a way to re-join her into conversion.

Anisidor: She collapsed into a prior act. Conversion requires capturing the substance in a reverse order.

Me: We will do it, in the right moment. We will reverse the platform.

Steve: That's too dangerous. First, we get out and then we will see. Maybe we have to consult the Oracle first. Let's see what the Water Brooks offer.
We all agree.
Neil: What the hell do they look like? I know only that they are dispersed. They keep changing directions.
Anisidor: No one is safe, even when he thinks so. A constant fragility of space. Intoxicating perfume of mystic bliss. But in truth they are only mirrors. Nothing more than mirrors. We must move into those dangerous waters, free from our faces.
Me: How is that possible?
Anisidor: I have no idea. But it is what I heard, a long time ago, when I was a sailor in the Great Green Sea.

Troy: The Water Brooks

Hierophile: Time's clock. Mirrors traversing existence. Dreams lie on dreams, like clouds lie on clouds. Dreams are eaten away, face after face. The whole of face production. Swim alone. Speak alone. Consume desire alone. It is a sea of loneliness. That's it. That's a good description. Fight is abandoned. Never fight yourself in the water. Leave it to cover you like a warm blanket of loving skin. Do you know what Desire is about? I never had an idea. I don't remember. A folly, I think. A needed folly. A sub-hydra of monstrous foetuses. They come out of every single body and fill the whole anatomy. No face, nothing; only a strong, demanding, feverish flesh. Incarnation takes place on bodies. Without a body there is no desire. Face is a killing individuality, where the body is a luminous unity. We belong to the body. Bodies are bound through analogy. Eyes. I need eyes. Without a gaze I have no desire. I must let my gaze's enchantment grasp the eye in a contact. The caresses of the eye traversed by an eye. Affection or affliction? Tormented by love.
Traveller: There is no such extension here. Love is a mythical space. A word of intensity. An intensifier. Joy liquidates in pleasure. Pleasure evaporates through carnal pores. Here we have only mirrors.
Hierophile: Shall I look?
Traveller: A mouse or a cat?
Me: She is devastating in her suffering, or am I wrong?
Traveller: She is sorry for her lost voice. She thought she had a beautiful voice. He said so. He admitted it.
Me: She pretended to have a chance. Did she really have one?

Traveller: Of course, her future. The future is a choice of chances.

Me: But it is a double nothingness, like a boat's float in a no shore sea.

Traveller: Hope. All comes back to the common. Hope. Please do not laugh. We never laugh about hopes; they are sacred. Even more than souls. Hopes are innocent dramas of existence.

Me: Is existence a hope, or a choice?

Traveller: The choice of hope.

Me: But what about evil?

Traveller: You mean human evil or nature's destructions?

Me: Both.

Traveller: Nature is incapable of evil. She has no choice, as such. She carries phenomena not moralities.

Me: Human, then.

Hierophile: The human condition is a terrible sickness.

Traveller: Do you have dreams, Hierophile?

Hierophile: Day dreams?

Traveller: No, dreams. Not scenarios for your life. I speak of dreams.

Hierophile: Occasionally.

Traveller: Let yourself move to sleep and dream. Dream and find a stream where your dream will merge. If it is vivid enough, it might come across a connection, then you will fall out of the grip and see the mirror. It is only one. It appears as many but it's only one. It reflects one and only possibility. It's a choice.

Hierophile: My desire fades.

Traveller: Do you seek desire? I thought that you were seeking tranquillity.

Me: Tranquillity is dead form; anguish is alive.

Traveller: What fun to speak to both of you. Anguish is lacking. Here, nothing is lacking. You have set up Theogony and your Protogonos took place.

Me: Correct.

Traveller: Narrate then. Let me know your story. I love to listen, as you already know, I am unable to see. Narrate.

Me: We started not from chaos. We decided to build a state machine. Then we created a tape of instances. We used an index. Every time a new state was switched in, a new reading was possible. Later we decided to make it simpler. A twofold situation. A Yes and a No. We added a rule. The rule was the initiative of reproduction. Next, we decided to add a validation system. By choosing Truth you reconditioned living. Non-Truth was leading to Nothingness. Finally, we decided to combine state machines and our twofold trees. The tape was a tree construction but, nonetheless, her proliferation, her growth, made her look more like a rhizome. That was the secret. So simple. You keep the machine, you redefine the tape. And see what happens. New possibilities. Linearity disappeared. We called the loop: Eternal Return. I can assure you; it's exactly that, except that a trouble appeared; it works in closed circles that are getting smaller and faster, like orbits fasten around the same star. Among them branches are coming to light; grow up, dry, or disappear, but are like shadowy dreams, ghost lives, clouds in ephemeral skies, the orbits are the sole reality.

Traveller: Wonderful, a Theogony all made by intellectualised mechanics.

Me: We call it Mehen.

Traveller: Lovely name.

Me: We think so.

Traveller: Tell me more.

Hierophile: It works like a factuality. It is stoned in past.

Traveller: Please, my dear Hierophile, let me laugh.

Hierophile: Let me continue. It is a past projected from the future.

Traveller: I can't stop laughing.

Hierophile: The now is a consummation. A fuel. Desire is articulated as reality.

Traveller: Desire for what?

Me: Wrong question.

Traveller: Speak. Explain.

Hierophile: Desire is only the fuel. There is nothing to be added. You could not add a *for*. It's not a protheses. It's only articulation. Like blood in a body. The foundation lies in the impulse to be.

Traveller: My dear, the impulse loses power; it fades if it is left alone to traverse the space.

Me: Here comes the orbital system. It keeps coherence in expense of death. As the orbit fastens and the speed accelerates; Death is the only possibility to win Entropy. The closed system needs a valve. It keeps killing in order to live. It is self-eating. Self-lacerating. Like a snake eating his own head.

Traveller: Ourovoros?

Me: Exactly. He eats himself. The tape moves infinitely but the state machine is a closed box. Every cell can be reproduced but it can also die. It's a dualistic cosmos although it has only one immanent substance. Like a point that splits to two curves, only to be able to join them again, back to their previous one. We are part of the split.

Traveller: It sounds complicated.

Me: It is not. It is simple. It is a matter of numbers. As numbers accumulate, it falls into phenomenal complication, but in principle, it's simple. One substance, many divisions.

Traveller: You said two.

Hierophile: Two are enough to split, by multiplications, into millions, trillions. The world's egg, the silvery egg in the Father's womb.

Traveller: You say that the Father is Darkness?

Hierophile: Flux. Streams of flux.

Traveller: You call me Father?

Hierophile: I call you Mother. I call you Eden. A space to cross, a territory in suspension until the day that it is crossed.

Traveller: Oh, you little light of absurdity. Stop speaking. I prefer the older versions. Where are my Titans? Where are my Erevos? Where are my Ophions and my Harpies? Where are my Oceanids? What a miserable platform of existence. Get your numbers and bathe fast in the streams before my Moirai bust you into my Ades.

Me: They can't. You know in the Brooks you have no other power than mirroring.

Traveller: Of course, I can. Passivity; it's not my substance; my mirrors are a primary reflection. Be careful. I can always mislead you.

Hierophile: You don't want that.

Traveller: No, I don't want that. I want to see where you are able to go; my no limits are my limit. Your restrained existence; your limited body is to me, like a tempting possibility of rephrasing my texture. My need to dream. Help me dream in your dreams.

Hierophile: I am afraid I have only nightmares.

Traveller: Don't be ungrateful dear. You have adventurous dreams.

Hierophile: I have a heart that is light. Pain does not exist. I forgot that I was in pain once.

Traveller to Hierophile: That's my promise, my dear Hierophile. That's my promise; until the next suffering, you will suffer not.

Traveller to Me: Troy, move to the Lacuna. She will wait for you. Be careful; you will come across a secondary reflection. Be aware. Pay attention.

Troy: The Lacuna

Anisidor: We came just in time; we lost Drusiana; we can't afford a second loss.

Me: The second reflection.

Neil: I suppose so.

Anisidor: We are coming close to the second reflection. Possibly it's time to solve the riddle. Look at her, dream after dream, illusion after illusion; she is getting more and more transparent, more and more white.

Steve: Her blood elucidates and makes real the being of his thought.

Me: A transient being. Ambiguity? Walled in her lonely existence.

Anisidor: I think she said so.

Me: She said also that she is both the Signifier and the Signified.

Anisidor: She said that he was only the Intermediate.

Neil: Under Wrath or Rage?

Anisidor: I think, she thought of his manners of conduct as humiliation or rejection, maybe both.

Steve: She accumulated discerned hopes.

Me: A parallel? An addition?

Anisidor: Two characters portraying a chance of happiness.

Neil: So, naïve?

Anisidor: So much in need. A continual process of self-making. She is self-begetting. From time to time she falls into despair. She demands inspiration. Exchange, seduction, inspiration. Her breath.

Neil: Does she want to control?

Anisidor: No, that would have made her completely unhappy. She demands a possibility. I am responsible for a possibility, she said.

Neil: What a stupid statement.

Anisidor: Of course, but she knew not what else to say.

Steve: We would rather create a chance than wait for one. Waiting relinquishes Hope.

Me: Yes that makes sense, but why claim responsibility?

Anisidor: Matter of strength. She has mixed up strength and dignity.

Steve: It feels decent to be strong.

Me: That makes sense too.

Neil: She was right, I think.

Anisidor: Do not forget Drusiana; from now on we must continue all together.

She is waiting for us. She is alone. She looks pale and her eyes are shining like the flip of bats in nocturnal waters. Such a strange place. The water is flowing up and then down, whirling and then infusing the night into a pool of wondering. She is there in the middle of this pondering, the transparency of a lonely flower. Yearning in her inner sadness. Grieving his sudden farewell.

Oracle: The mariners passed beyond the limit, didn't they?

Me: Yes, we passed, but in a loss of the female fruit. We lost Drusiana.

Oracle: A surrendered dream.

Me: A dreadful reality.

Oracle: There comes the day, the return of the lost. The wheel will come full circle. Sanctify the innocent. The effigy is a mental space.

Me: Shall we function the recognition?

Oracle: Not yet.

Oracle: The Lacuna works toward diverted ends. She doesn't care for your space.

Me: I am afraid of the circumstances. They are given; we do not create them. We play but the lands move forward into recoil.

Oracle: You play on others' performance.

Steve moved to the edge.

Steve: Look, she is formed by limbs.

We all stared in the direction of his gaze. The Lacuna moved, touching all edges with trembling limbs.

Me: The Hydra. That must be the notion of Hydra. Not a creature, not a pool, but the will of expansion.

Steve: You are right, Troy.

Oracle: Please there is no fear here, simply an epic reporting to the angel. The rock will be displaced softly, and the rays will fill her savage existence. The Gorgon gives birth to the winged egg.

Anisidor: The primordial creature.

Oracle: Yes, the primal pool. Limbs as disconnected members of a body are falling like a rain. Blood dew. Fuel of cosmos. From here on, I read not the omens; I have no power of remembering future.

Anisidor: Let's continue then.

Oracle: How? I am going to contradict myself. The uncertainty is so vast. I am afraid.

Anisidor: You said that there is no fear here.

Oracle: For you. For me it is intense, like a day without a sound.

Neil: We didn't fight our way here for nothing.

Me: Wait, take a deep breath and move to the unpredictable. We will be here to help you.

Oracle: Is it justified?

Neil: We only demand victory.

Oracle: Victory is pure justification. Am I capable of it?

Anisidor: Devouring your first self doesn't mean that you don't have a second. You consumed only a version. Move to the next. Disguise. Remember, all is about the metaphor. Touch all edges. Take all shapes. Move. We must find Drusiana. It all comes to her. We need her; otherwise we will be still, and we cannot fight the unpredictable in stillness.

Hierophile: Coronal Light, the Nucleus in Transaction of Transference

Oracle: I am near, but I can't see. My body is passing from Neptunian transformations. He is astonishing in his colour of fever. Open scars. No blood. Fish are dropping in their agony of birth. As I can't master my fearful skin, I develop a serpent's skin. I have space to ascend but not a distance. I have space to descend but not a horizon. I have only the possibility to recoil in myself. Obey or disobey, it makes no difference. An inwards attraction. A cage. I am Affirmation. It all comes to the same end. Myself. A vortex or a vertex? I am changing skin; the old falls in astral delusions; the new ascends in astral illusions. No matter, no spirit, no creature is out of my reach. The egg encapsulates winds, earths, waters, and fires, but entering the womb triggers the only entity, the unified seed. Before that we must permit the Gathering. Lacuna is his vertex of being. His spasm of existence. Lonely like a foetus, lonely like dissolute Eros. Limbs featuring limbs. No human evaporation, no human submission. Limbs, lonely as a mutilated corpse, demand a breath in a pure vanity. Such is the chorus. The degrees of vibration are causing the numbers sequence. At the four falls into human abstraction. While at twelve forms the full zodiac. Watch at the three, the circle revaluates all.
Neil: What did she say?
Steve: I have no idea.
Neil: A prophecy?
Troy: She steals, I think.
Oracle: I have stolen the divine proportion on your behalf. And yet I would not be punished any more, since punishment became indifferent to mother. She fed me the divine proportion of her own will. I was not a theft. It all comes to the entrance permission.
Anisidor: Watch for tomorrow. Encryption. That's our identity. The Lacuna is an illustration. Deliberate ambiguity. It works on one and only level. Self-appropriation. The Hidden, the Veiled reconsiders its own dimension; sometimes, arises like sea foam and others dwell in the deep.
Oracle: Her life breathes away as softly as in a festivity of sweet dreams. To find

Drusiana you must search in the Dragon's land. Lacuna is our permission. We must fall into her limbs.

Troy: How is that possible?

Oracle: Help me, Troy, to rehearse the opacity. Help me to light up the Sun himself, his body's chest bright chestnut; a silver circle shone between his brows. From his brow, branched horns of even length like the crescent of the horned Moon when her disk is cloven in twain. He is now cast out in the deep, keeping her soft breath in unawakening sleep, but when his skin gets wet, the Lacuna can break into waves and lift up the land of fires.

Anisidor: Oh, my sweet silent melody, she is sleeping in the bitterness of his ferocity.

Neil: How the hell can we make his skin wet?

Steve: I think I know.

Anisidor: Bearing her bridal gifts, fair leaves and flowers and sacred soil.

Oracle: The holy verses.

Steve: With his waters that the wild olives drunk.

Anisidor: Homage to the poet. Homage to the torch that has been given from the Muse.

Oracle: I walked this path and I got burned from humiliation. Not again, never again. Find another way, Steve, find me another gate and bring Drusiana back with us.

Neil: Let's fall then. Let's make it simple. We fall into her hands and see what the Lacuna offers.

Neil pushes me in with one movement. Steve, Troy and Anisidor throw themselves after us. And there we are in the First Aletheia.

Troy: She said so; she said that we are into the first Aletheia. But she didn't say what the Aletheia was about. We had to find out for ourselves.

Oracle: The riddle, we came to the riddle. I remember it's a homonym, but of what? Of what?

Mithras: Are these woes wept? Are these tales of grief forgotten? Mourn over the human agony. Mourn over the wonderings of the heart. The rocky city. Wounded in many sorrows, gathered the bones of all into one golden urn.

Troy: Thebes. Their celestial counterpart. The longing of his poisonous swallowing. We are in his belly. Got up inside like fish for his supper.

Oracle: Fire up the torch, begetting the resonances of night gale. Oh no, resonate the melody of partition. Oh no, rewind his time back to the stone. Half of his body unable to move. Then his skin will get wet from his own sweat.

Neil: We cannot kill him, but we could always bury him, returning him to his first condition.

Steve: Bring him closer to the primal orientation.

Troy: Wonderful, then return him to the Mother and bring back Menath. Reformat.

Steve: The encryption is recounting from the last branch to the former, to the beginning; a simple mirroring stage. Like a retina that absorbs light into reversals.

Oracle: Renounce orientation by a repercussive echo; replace my liver with opaque fluid; on rush fatal my illusion's flash.

Menath: My dear Hierophile, you lost so much time forgetting to count. Forgetting who you are.

Oracle: I never forgot; it is only that I am uncertain. I have no idea what to count and why. I mean, I try, but then all that seems absurd and I lose the meaning. Count is an endless process.

Menath: But my dear, you must find the relation.

Oracle: That is an even bigger problem. Relation to what? Please, I am useless with numbers.

Menath: Not at all; you are so close that you lose the picture. Take a distant eye and then let it spring like a basket of gold carrying narcissus, hyacinth and violet upon the creeping thyme. The yoke. Save the daughter of Inachus. Argus has sleepless eyes. From his red blood a bird rejoiced in a flower bright colour: The golden vessel. My Hierophile, get the golden vessel. May the Graces be with you.

So, he speaks, and Hierophile finds herself on the back of the Bull, but this time, she has the yoke. He is taken by surprise. A yoked animal.

Hierophile: You must compromise. Io will inhabit Thebes, a queen in the vast lands of the upper realm, but you will drive me to the land of the Dragon. You, my golden vessel, for my journey to eternity.

He is somehow amazed like he wants to be captured, like he is expecting to be tamed. But I know well that he pretends. I have a pure victory.

Mithras: No. You had a predestined victory but here comes the biggest of your efforts. Here is the Dragon land. Get your crew and fight your way.

Troy: The Dragon Land (The Automaton Defying Itself)

Me: A pulsed emission, a highly magnetised rotating density. The atomic clock. The moment of inertia is highly reduced. An angular momentum and the whole collapses. The rotational energy emits firing beams. The field will accelerate, the cloud gas will explore; we must pass fast. Time is accurate. It will split in its binary.

Steve: A Doppler shift?

Steve moves to the console with obvious uneasiness.
Steve: The pulses are frequent. It is moving closer. We turn to the weaker field; we win time. We have a companion in circular orbit.
Neil: A periastron.
Neil speaks with admiration.
Steve: Time dilation. Time shifts. The matter flows into accretion disk.
Troy: The Bull's crescent moon is now full. A parallax. We must fly on the lines until we reach the curve. All components undergo mutuality.
Neil: Is it a danger of gravitational pull?
Steve: I think, a transfer of mass due to the stellar wind. A symbiotic luminous red Dragon. The perturbation is strong; it might be rejected, and we fall into hydrogen fusion. The Stymphalian birds may appear during inhalation.
Neil: I know; they are clusters in the form of swans.
Steve: Remember he never sets. Thuban, the head of the serpent, is visible only to the Pyramis. We have no other option than to perform a progenitor and capture him by freezing, before he changes state.
Me: *Eydaimonia.* Here is our Dragon Land.
We walk with light feet. A profusion, an odour of intoxicating perfume.
Neil: What does that mean?
Me: I have no idea, but it feels like an essence.

I am delighted. Suns are running the sky and moons are waxing their orbits into radiated rays. Beauty is pondering and, as an accidental source, constitutes the tangible response. Real or Unreal wasn't the question. No, the question was changed long ago. Situated already in ephemeris time, we walk under falling sun flakes, touching each other's hands in treasured silence. I stare, searching eyes and lips, searching breath and skin, and I see flowers of jelly; our arteries are pulling and pushing blood inside crystalline vases. Strange qualities are spreading from marvelous spectrums and striking clearness.

He seized, a great voice: 'Behold.'

The voice of a thunderbolt of augmented flame, forsaken in the wildness. Fiery eyes, blazes of pure intelligence, flares of glorious swords bestowed their impression on us.

'Welcome to my lonely existence. I crossed the waters and flew up in a whirlwind, but I lost my mantle in a vineyard. Four were my worlds, Wind, Storm, Fire and Stillness. But look, the bee swarm is right here, the Golden Bee resides, completely unmoved. Where are your hives?'

He continued, in an alighted voice: 'Was night and darkened all the land of Nile.

Things turned transitory and vain. Dissolution. My sad exclusion. But there was a wide passage. A passage as wide as the openings of my wings. An after time. An optic tube of radiant light. The seed: an endless gratitude. The pearl. A solemn bird fragrance of delightful earth. The Golden Bee sits on the bloom, extracting liquid sweet. Where are your hives?'

He continued, in a violent voice: 'I desired to grasp the eternal. Dreams framed in private cells, while fear lacked visibility. The fountain. Speed contained the Milky Way. An instruction not to spare the fruit. Pour and receive intellect. The Golden Bee in the dance of the smelling sweet. Where are my hives?'

He continued, in a soaring song: 'Transgressing the tree. Fluid mass. Spread branches hung over voids. I, the attribute to the circle's swiftness. Me, the affirmation of motion in the heavens. The Golden Bee, wide circuiting of flesh. Where are my hives?'

He continued, in a soft lullaby: 'Invite the exceeded human, the inhabitant. Progressive, retrograde, or standing? Still roaming without end. Each tree a guide of presence. Where are my hives?'

He then seized a tremendous voice: 'I warn you. Rise to the Union, elevate to the Nuptial. The Herdsman waits under the mother tree. Where are my hives?'

Hierophile: The Oracle's Song

Rise in me my soul, vast lands are my love
Bathe in me my soul, profound seas are my love
The lotus emerald pearl yearning for your precious scent
The moon's crimson flux longing for your dear dwell
Like the strong winged bird carry me to the branches of life
The guardian of the scarlet temple lights my dream of splendor
The pomegranate's jewel stirs again the Great Green Sea
Touch gently the earth's chant as the sacred tree awakes its fiery growth in time

Troy: The Vineyard

'I was among the
            captives by the river, that the heavens were opened,
I looked, and, behold, a whirlwind came out of the North,
            a great cloud, and a fire unfolding itself, and a brightness

was about it, and out of the midst thereof as the colour of
amber, out of the midst of the fire.

Now as I beheld the living creatures, behold one wheel upon
the earth by the living creatures, with his four faces.

The appearance of the wheels and their work was like unto the
colour of a beryl: and they four had one likeness: and their
appearance and their works were as if a wheel in the middle
of a wheel.

When they went, they went upon their four sides: and they
turned not when they went.

As for their rings, they were so high that they were dreadful;
and their rings were full of eyes round about them four.

And when the living creatures went, the wheels went by them:
and when the living creatures were lifted up from the earth,
the wheels were lifted up'

The time has come; the day of trouble is near. The wheel is in the midst of the wheel.

'And these are the goings out of the city on the north side,
four thousand and five hundred measures.
and three gates northward;

And at the east side four thousand and five hundred: and three
gates;

And at the south side four thousand and five hundred measures:
and three gates;

At the west side four thousand and five hundred, with their
three gates.'

Me: It is round about 18,000 measures; the hives of heavens.

Steve: The angles among successive elements are equivalent to a rotation by a number of turns equal to 1.618 as the limit ratio.

Me: A wave background?

Steve: Thermal equilibrium is falling. We have infinite inputs but 2 empowers infinity to limited possibility, with 3 gates in our availability we reduced in 23 classes which can affect 38,976 wires to reproduce the functions.

Neil: Form a continuous system then. Block also the initial conditions.

Steve: For 4 sides, 4,500 measures and 3 gates for each side. That means 4 sides and 13,500 wires for each side, the whole 54,000.

Me: Is it an approximation? Is it reducible to our possession? Wheels, faces, rings and eyes, what is all that about?

Steve: Shall we calculate the reversals?

Steve calculates the reversals and applies them in a new class of arrangement; a combination of the three dimensions of physical space and the three dimensions of velocity space. We reach the Promised Land. Dry frost earth. Accumulation of sand. Troy has a tube for breathing. The seed he says. The fucking seed.

Steve: We are lost. Miscalculation. We fell into the Irreversible. The hives; we forgot the cells are zygotes, formless at the beginning; then they figure out wheels.

Neil: Yes. Yes, I remember, wheels, faces, rings and eyes. And on the top are zygotes and they divide two by two to four. Not only that; present is an addition of two clusters, both past and future. We messed it up. That's the point.

We answer to the riddle with half of a homonym.

Steve: No, a half-homonym doesn't exist. We simply failed.

Me: Not completely. At least we are on the ground.

Neil: Back to the beginning; only this time we remember.

Steve: That's even worse. We were already distressed enough.

Me: Where are Anisidor and the Oracle?

Steve: Captives by the river. Whirling around in the great cloud.

Neil: That means...?

Steve: We lost them, but we are performing, are not dismantled.

Neil: Shall we get them back?

Steve: How? We are thrown.

Me: I have an idea, Neil. Steve, you remember? In Heliopolis. The Egg.

Steve: Ok, so what?

Me: We shall repeat the vistas of the game. We were deceived by the explanation. We failed in our plan, but we can always risk a possibility. We related our activity to the being to come, while the limit of this being was encapsulated in the past. We must re-enter. We must form the link. The second aid.

Steve: All right, I have left an open margin just in case of misfortune.

Me: Great Steve, that's fantastic.

Neil is under frantic enthusiasm.

Neil: We fall into surpassing; get the time-beings on the table. Those are dices made by hyle, warm like sunbeams.

Steve: Shall we use annihilation?

Me: No, better to transcend the activity.

Steve: Isn't that dangerous?

Me: There is always the possibility of losing ourselves.

Steve: But that is already happening.

Me: Exactly.

Steve: We search for the crack, the slipping out, the entry for the self-orienting game.

Me: Our self in conscious evolution.

Steve: Either time will absorb everything, or we get being out of the dream.

Neil: My sweethearts, it is just an explosive celebration; get into the game light-hearted.

Hierophile: The Decoding or Representations

Component 1: The Gambling Table.

The conjunction. A topography of the circumstances. Frame of the limits. We call it the Table. The Table is given. *Let's see what constitutes the Table:* Nine components, or elements, including its own map, a spiral of appearances related to each other, predestined to unify all the other elements. It is the structure over the elements and it is also called the Plan. The living material, it is founded as a mode of its own existence or as the progressive sequence and it is called the seed or the hylozoic prominence. The table partakes in all. Formation doesn't necessarily imply difference. The table is not interpretation, but demonstration. The immutable condition.

Component 2: The Dices.

A position. Providing a vehicle to the chance. A procession to proceed. Surpassing despite the weight of limits, expanding despite the closure of forces. Paving the way and forming the way. The means for real movement.

Component 3: Immanence.

Threads of episodes. The apparatus. The transmission system. The whole viewed as energy.

Component 4: Consolidate.

Precise sense of establishment. The crystallised body of the apparatus after being liquidated into specific energy. The worked material. Renovated eternity.

Component 5: She Loves.

The great commencement thrown back in the table. Unexpectedly taking hold. The unity as aggregation of the parallel interpellation. Conflagration.

Component 6: Incoherence.

The second appearance or transition. The struggle against interpellation. The self-enclosed totality, hovering to the infinite. The impact, the designation of particulars and the breaking of particulars. Separation in alienated wholeness.

Component 7: Communication.
The battlefield. Subjectivity grasps the eternity. Affirm myself by indexing to the other's affirmation. Circuitry.
Component 8: Randomness.
The effect. Abandoned in self-conception.
Component 9: Rolling On.
Future anteriority. The re-convergence. Neither back to the beginning, nor abandoning the reflective action. Evolution reverses in immortality. Time relapses in annulations.

'Troy, get the resorts,' *Steve shouts in full action.* 'We face a revolt on the accomplished. The egg emerges but as constraint. Reinforce the contact. Find the constant, not the law. Turn primary tendency to chance. Form the time–beings. Fast, hurry up. Now. The aid is in the form of an illuminating letter. Read it. It contains the preconditions. The prerogatives. Get it. It is a flight on a victorious horse. Form the armies immediately and get her out.'

Horus and Hystaspes in their bridal bed mimicking the time before

Hystaspes: I wished your body in my arms.
Horus: I wished my hands around your waist, touching your spine softly.
Hystaspes: I wished your eyes in mine.
Horus: I wished my gaze, bathing smoothly in your darkness.
Hystaspes: Galloping into passion. Fall. Fall in me.
Horus: I am here.
Hystaspes: Are you?
Horus: Certainly.
Hystaspes: I am spinning. The river never stops. A circular movement. An orbit without centre.

Hystaspes: The Sacred Armies (The Oracle Delivered or Hierophile's Formation)

He sent his angels to the Down. The sacred armies of the godly children, those that the great Sepulchre of the Woven did free. Immortal rays where fiction's light combats the glorious lands of the concealed. My poor child, insanity stroked his tender soul when life was forming her brightness. Sweet like the odour of heavenly aurora, he was unfit for the battle, an ideal of purity. He had no language; he knew not what the world was about. He was lonely in his courage to be. He was my child.

'Perform my destiny,' I said.

Angel's blossom laugh. Angel's sorrow eyes. He smiled and kissed me by touching his lips to mine. His small hand, a bird's egg, warm within its pulse of being. Sweet child against the sunbeams smiled and all vanished in dust. But there was a Rune, a Sigil, a Leaf; gold and white as the fabric of snow in the fields of the clay sun. The broken balance made a new terra under the forests of the gentle winds. Powerless in my weakness, pierced in my heart, wounded by my fear, armed with grief's shivering bullets: words of shadowy colours, distressed in my thought, I asked for aid; and there she came, beautiful solemn fragrance charging air all over earth, mastering the tribe of dreams; my mother in her graceful recompense. Longing for love, she sang a song, then she gave to my son the matter and the image. Play my sweetheart, she said. Play and be, walk and fly. Throw your dice in the uncertainty. Untroubled and un-aging for all days, keep each other. Sheep and fowls seal your unity, floating as ever, woe upon woe.

Hystaspes: The Riddle is burning, unresolved. Did praise and conquest the Fortune's ride.

Troy: Astonished and amazed, we stood, not having been able for the assembly. From mouth to mouth, from eye to eye, forth passed forth, the fear and terror. So many sheep and fowls; weak, feeble, small.

Hystaspes: Among the rest he runs. And in small space, small time, great wonders brought.

Troy: Astonished and amazed, we stood, not having been able for the assembly. Each one lifts up his sword, advances his shield.

Hystaspes: He cleaves; he tears; he falls down.

Troy: Smoke and flow through all the purple field. We forgot all of our names. Strange flyers spread the signs of Dilation.

Hystaspes: He is coming swift.

Troy: That all ages be your love and sweet accord.

Hystaspes: Did he come late?

Troy: No. On the contrary.

Hystaspes: Let him fight so that he would escape.

Troy: When all seemed lost, he won.

Hystaspes: As a lion in fury and disdain.
Troy: Their wounds, their hurts, forgot both death and life.
Hystaspes: Alone saved her guides?
Troy: Half mad, half amazed, fled from friends and opened wide.
Hystaspes: Dream's last word is love.
Troy: She revives, moist with her own tears.
Hystaspes: Behold.
Troy: Behold of the river's streams.
Hystaspes: Life won the fight.

Troy: The Argument

The sacred armies were a strange idea for deliverance. The notion was to take Drusiana back with us; thus, we had to revitalise the Oracle named Hierophile. We couldn't make it to the Gathering without them. Anisidor was a milestone; we needed his swarming. The sudden was the duplication; the interference caused noise and we lost the signal's transmission; but here was a fallen element, a Knight, Steve's providence; that was a brilliant idea; it worked as a zygote and paired the Oracle, creating her fondness of ambition. Then we marched straight on the host and Neil re-established the Shires of Existence, what previously we had called Time-Beings. We stretched backwards but not on the same plane; instead, we won the fight and succeeded to get to the commons from each side and form the Era of the Gathering by mixing the four worlds into one. The Oracle became the Terrain. While the Knight was the movement to the Profound. The consequence evolved into understanding of the Self-Reference, the evidence that we could form a response anew. One world is our time's possibility: Our world in an infinity of appearances.
We solved the riddle by deliverance.

Troy: The Gathering

Hierophile: World of imagination. Can all be called real? Transition works silently. The line of fires is broken, and their smoke rises darkly upwards. *Eleusis.* It is raining; I am alone in a room. Tranquil. Water firmament in exultation? Redefining myself. Fusion into unity. The circumstances crystallising instances in annulment. Is it accomplished? Compromising the exception. The supports? Inflexible to tenant the message. The gathering on which they have eluent inclined in the principal vain act: Pay oneself;

forgetting that symbols traverse the world. Opened then, the subterranean ocean. The four wings; a flux of mighty waters. Cities, people and everything else has perished. Plants and rocks turned towards the ascension. Products of an audacious nature. Puissance of their personal fantasies. Their miserable hearts. full of hatred, were too small to hold the ethereal. The exterior? Nothing can sustain his own force. They received the discourse but instead they prepared an inferior region. Fragmentation. The development of the first inversion. Desire to unfold its own warmth. Conflated, circumnavigating the globe: The hurrying impact shifted from the upheaval to an endorsed common stance of meaning, leading to a strengthened amendment. But that was only a tale of woe. The shell was intact. Inaccessible? I do not know; is it human or an entrance? The private eye of heavens a case of limits? Unrest. All are perfectly adapted to their end. When he said so? I don't remember. What about motion? The hidden base of the human structure. Is that an irony? No longer intervenes; that's his secret. Not an absence, but a disappearance in transmission. We have been blocked out. The conflict generates its own motive. A grave defect. A halt. Hardly by accident, I think; a voluntary turn.

Neil: To whom is she speaking?
Me: I think, to the Dead.
Steve: She borrows words, not illusions.
Me: I know.
Neil: What about the third aid?
Me: A curious sacrament of auto-suggestion.
Neil: What does that mean?
Me: The sign of the fish.
Steve: A ratio?
Me: Probably.
Steve: A controlling ratio. *Omnis Obscuritas.*
Me: The pairing is said to call for inscribed reflection.
Steve: The conjoint in a new emphasis.
Neil: The metaphor is taking hold.
Me: The current's accomplishment in primary occurrence; the birth of the unreal.
Steve: The contact. She establishes the contact.
With timely pride above the Egyptian vale.
    'Mother,' she said, 'I will undertake to do this deed.'
    Nile's waves to fertile slime outweigh and overflow each plane and lowly dale: Spreading himself full upon her huge heaps of mud, he leaves his fruitful seed; then

her son from his ambush, stretches forth his left hand all over the Great Green Sea and rejoices greatly in spirit, and there are the shining gates and the unmovable threshold of heavens having unending roots grown of itself: Cosmos reform; bringing on the night's star and yearning for love.

Omphalos or the Ideo Fugiet

Over the waters
gliding flare, upheld and shone
amid heaven and earth where the sky's glass breeds
facing the moon's shadow and her pivot
Fearless duration runs in the presence of necessity the mental velocity
Addressing the melting splendour
opening the patterned pass,
growing fervidly, swarming eagerness and clouds
swarming ridges and horizons
the flowered branch recalls both proportions and principle.
While the light's silk outwards the spirit's brightness
And I say:
I see another Mind and I, Mind, understand.

Acknowledgments

I would like to express my gratitude to the British Council & Kingston Writing School for the publication of the book.

I am very thankful to the MA students Jade Grocott, Holly Roberts, Lidia Trifonova and Yulianna Permyakova and their course leader Emma Tait for the excellent work on this book.

I am deeply grateful and greatly indebted to Dr David Rogers for his generous assistance, advice and support during the entire preparation of the manuscript for publication.

Glossary Of Names And History

'Ει καλως ειρηται το λαϑε βιωσας': Greek, 'It is good to live without being noticed,' Epictetus

'Σιβυλλα τι ϑελεις?': Greek, 'Sybil what do you wish for?'

Aletheia: Latinised Greek, 'Truth'. Used here in the Platonic sense. It is also a hint for alethic modalities (i.e., necessity, contingency, possibility and impossibility).

Ancillae: Latin, 'Auxilliary.'

Anisidor: Latinised Greek, 'Broken gifts'

Astro: Latinised Greek, 'Star'.

Bennu: Ancient Egyptian deity linked with the sun, creation, and rebirth, worshipped at Heliopolis.

Bythos: Latinised Greek, 'Depth or Profundity'. Used here as in Gnostics, Aeon (Pleroma or Emanation).

Ceteris paribus: Latin, 'Everything else being normal.'

Chora: Latinised Greek, 'Place, location, region, country.' Used here as in Plato, Timaeus ('Mother, receptable')

Disypostaton: Latinised Greek, 'Double essence.'

Ektases: Latinised Greek, 'Area, stretching, volume, extent, spread'

Er: The myth of Er (Plato, Republic)

Eudaimonia: Latinised Greek, 'Happiness, flourishing'. Used here as in Aristotle.

Heliopolis: Latinised Greek, 'City of the Sun'.

Homoion: Latinised Greek, 'Having the same quality or essence'

Ideo fugiet a te Omnis Obscuritas: Latin, 'For this reason all obscurity shall vanish'.

Io: The holy caw, mistress of Zeus (in the form of The Bull). Daughter of Inachos (the river god) she arrived in Nile and had a child with Zeus. She is also the founder of Thebes. The ancient Phocians were celebrating Io when the sun transited in the sign of Taurus. The goddess Isis (the three-coloured caw: white, black, purple) in ancient Egypt.

Krasis: Latinised Greek, 'mixing, blending'. In the text Krasis is used as a reference to the intelligible fountains. Souls are also called fountains of motions. Crater be the cause of souls, the receptacle of their fabrication and the generative monad of them (Proclus: Theology of Plato).

Kymvala pepwka: Latinised Greek, 'I drunk the drums' (Orphic verse)

Matralia: Festival for the Latin goddess Mater Matuta

Methexis: Latinised Greek (see also Methectics), 'Sharing or participating.' The relation between a particular and a form in Plato.

Mnevis: Hellenised name of an ancient Egyptian bull god which had its centre of worship at Heliopolis.

Ourovoros (Ouroboros): Ancient Greco-Egyptian symbol depicting a serpent or dragon eating its own tail.

Pileus: A ceremony for freeing a slave in Ancient Rome.

Protogonos: Latinised Greek, 'Primordial'. According to Hesiod, Nyx fertilised by Ether, gave birth to a silver egg; from the egg Eros came into life. His other names are: Phanes, Metis, Herikepaios.

Salva veritate: Latin, 'With truth saved.'

Sellos: The name of the forest, a name chosen as a reminder to Selloi. Selloi were inhabitants of Epirus in ancient Greece (Dodona region) and priests of the Dodona Oracle.

Servus non habet personam: Latin, 'A slave has no persona'

Seven priests: The rulers of the world, the seven planets (Gnostic).

Sybils: Oracular women believed to possess prophetic powers in ancient Greece. Sabbe (in her role as Sybil) passed the Great Green Sea. Wanderer, from Libya to Cumean and then to Tibur where she changed her name to Albunea.

Sympeplegmenon: Latinised Greek, 'Consist of many but impossible to divide', as in Aristotle

Theasis: Latinised Greek, 'View, Sight, Scenery'.

Theogony: Latinised Greek, 'The genealogy or birth of the gods'

Toxon: Latinised Greek, 'Bow'

References

Aeschylus, Oresteia: Are these woes wept? ... the wonderings of heart

Artaud, A., I have done with the Judgement of god: You can tie me up if you wish, but there is nothing more useless than an organ. My mind became a place of refuge, a sanctuary.

Artaud, A., On the Balinese theatre: I am the passive voice

Artaud, A., On the Balinese theatre: The Cosmos is moved by ever active sacred lines

Bakunin, M., God and the state, 1882: Sacrificing the living men

Blake, W., Jerusalem: Pleasure and pain shall complete the day

Blake, W., Jerusalem: The rocky city. Wounded in many sorrows. Gathered the bones of all into one golden urn

Blake, W., Proverbs of Hell: Let man wear... immortal hand or eye.

Emerald Tablet, Chrysogonus Polydorus, Nuremberg 1541: Ideo fugiet a te omnis obscuritas

Euripides, The Bacchae: Say to her that Bacchius freed you

Heraclitus of Ephesus: Humidity is Death or Eros

Heraclitus of Ephesus: Now you have died and now you have come into being

Hermetica. CODEX VI, Selection made from James M. Robinson, ed., The Nag Hammadi Library, revised edition. HarperCollins, San Francisco, 1990: I see another Mind,..And I, Mind, understand

Hölderlin, F., Hyperion: Fate mastered me and then Thundered

Homer, Odyssey: A fine line was keeping horizon like stem in her fingers

Keats, J., Isabella; or, the pot of Basil, A story from Boccaccio-LIII: And she forgot the stars...new morn she saw not

Keats, J., La Belle Dame Sans Merci. A Ballad: I see a lily on the brow, With anguish moist and fever dew.

Maimonides, Guide for the perplexed: Lost his mantle in a vineyard

Milton, J., Paradise Lost: From the North to call Decrepit Winter, from the South to bring Solstitial summer's heat

Moreau, Gustave, Jupiter et Semele, 1894 & Leda, 1865: Mysterious envelop

Moschus, 150BC: His body's chest bright chestnut ... cloven in twain

Nietzsche F., Beyond Good and Evil: Original sin coupled with the innate divinity of mankind

Nietzsche F., Human all too Human: It is the power of the one that kills the will of the many

Nietzsche, F., Human, all too human: Not being birds how do you propose to nest on an abyss

Orphic hymn: The son of beautiful Aether and my tender love

Pindar, Pythian: For I also dreamed that I am of your blessed race

Shelley, P., Prometheus Unbound: I didn't come to save you…To love and bear; to hope till Hope creates.

Shelley, P., Prometheus Unbound: Living shapes upon … all love

Song of Songs: Let him kiss me with the kisses of his mouth

Songs of Ascent, Mandaean scriptures, Ginza: Until I reach the watch …water brooks

Spengler, Oswald, The Decline of the West: The woman is the Oracle itself, and it is Time …devotion be kept within limits

St John: Book of Revelation: She is clothed with the sun, with the moon under her feet, and on her hand a garland of twelve stars

Tasso, Torquato, Jerusalem delivered, 1581: Astonished and … life won the fight

The Bible, King James version. Book 26: Ezekiel: I was among the…three gates.

Valery, P., Crisis of the Mind, 1919: Horrors would have never to kill so many…clear and pitiless

Valery, P., Crisis of the Mind, 1919: We had long heard tell of whole …same fragility as life

Valery, P., Crisis of the Mind, 1919: We have foreseen a gradual change …could dismay them

Virgil, Aeneid: Silent is the deep sky and the breezes are still; ocean hushes his waters into calm

Virgil, The eclogues: The Heliconian spring on frail foundations lay

Whitman, W., Leaves of Grass: Up then noble soul! Put on thy jumping shoes which are intellect and love

Whitman, W., Leaves of Grass: What are the roots that clutch, what branches grow

About The Author

Athena Gaga lives in Athens. Holds an MA degree in Developmental and Learning Disabilities and a BEng in Informatics. Worked as a senior designer in the telecommunications sector both in Greece and abroad and later on as a teacher in informatics in public high schools in Greece. She has attended the British Council, in partnership with Kingston Writing School, International Creative Writing Summer School held in Athens the years 2015, 2016 & 2017. Two of her short stories appeared in the collections of 2016 and 2018, 'The best of the Kingston writing school & British council international creative writing summer school'. Mehen is her first published novella.

About Kingston University Press

Kingston University Press has been publishing high-quality commercial and academic titles for over ten years. Our list has always reflected the diverse nature of the student and academic bodies at the university in ways that are designed to impact on debate, to hear new voices, to generate mutual understanding and to complement the values to which the university is committed.

Increasingly the books we publish are produced by students on the MA Publishing and BA Publishing courses, often working with partner organisations to bring projects to life. While keeping true to our original mission, and maintaining our wide-ranging backlist titles, our most recent publishing focuses on bringing to the fore voices that reflect and appeal to our community at the university as well as the wider reading community of readers and writers in the UK and beyond.

@KU_press

This book was edited, designed, typeset and produced by students on the MA Publishing course at Kingston University, London.

To find out more about our hands-on, professionally focused and flexible MA and BA programmes please visit:

www.kingston.ac.uk
www.kingstonpublishing.wordpress.com
@kingstonjourno

www.ingramcontent.com/pod-product-compliance
Lightning Source LLC
LaVergne TN
LVHW011212080426
835508LV00007B/752